Catching Bass Like a Pro

By Steve Price with Guy Eaker

FALCON®

A FALCON GUIDE®

Falcon® Publishing is continually expanding its list of recreational guidebooks. All books include detailed descriptions, accurate maps, and all information necessary for enjoyable trips. You can order extra copies of this book and get information and prices for other Falcon® books by writing Falcon, P.O. Box 1718, Helena, MT 59624, or by calling toll-free 1-800-582-2665. Also, please ask for a copy of our current catalog. Visit our website at www.Falcon.com or contact us by e-mail at falcon@falcon.com.

Printed in the United States of America.

1 2 3 4 5 6 7 8 9 0 MG 04 03 02 01 00

Cover photo: Steve Price
All black-and-white photos by the author unless otherwise noted.

Project Editor: Peggy O'Neill-Mcleod
Production Editor: Patrick Straub
Copyeditor: Brigid Wilson
Book design by A Page Turner
Cover Design by Michael Cutter

Library of Congress Cataloging-in-Publication Data

Eaker, Guy.
    Catching bass like a pro / by Steve Price with Guy Eaker.
       p.cm.
    ISBN 1-58592-082-7
       1. Bass fishing. I. Price, Steve, 1947- II. Title.

    SH681.E14 2001
    799.1'773—dc21

                                    00-064644

CAUTION
Outdoor recreational activities are by their very nature potentially hazardous. All participants in such activities must assume responsibility for their own actions and safety. The information contained in this guidebook cannot replace sound judgment and good decision-making skills, which help reduce exposure, nor does the scope of this book allow for the disclosure of all the potential hazards and risks involved in such activities.

Learn as much as possible about the outdoor recreationl activities in which you participate, prepare for the unexpected, and be cautious. The reward will be a safer and more enjoyable experience.

 Text pages printed on recycled paper.

CONTENTS

Dedication iv

Acknowledgments v

1   How It All Began 1

2   A Bass Is a Bass Is a Bass 7

3   Tricks for Finding Bass 15

4   Five Quick Patterns to Remember 21

5   Water Temperature and Bass Behavior .29

6   Bass and the Weather 37

7   Lure Presentation 45

8   Spinnerbaits Shallow and Deep 53

9   Probing the Bottom with Jigs 63

10   Playing with Plastics 71

11   Power Fishing with Plastic Tubes 83

12   Getting More from Your Crankbaits 89

13   Fun with Topwater Lures 96

14   Going After Trophy Bass 105

15   Turning Pro 113

16   Obtaining Sponsorships 121

17   Mental Attitude: Your Most Important Tool 129

Index 136

About the Author 142

DEDICATION

To Valerie and Travis, in hopes fishing will provide as much enjoyment in their lives as it has in mine.
—Steve Price

To my father, Earl Eaker, who was not only a great bass fisherman himself, but who spent thousands of hours on the water teaching me the basics; to my mother, Bertha Eaker, who was always there when we came home; and to my wife, Pat, and my children, Guy Jr. and Carla, for all their support through the years.
—Guy Eaker

ACKNOWLEDGMENTS

Although this book has two authors, a number of individuals played major roles in the project. Some of them never realized they were even involved, but their contributions cannot be overlooked.

Among these are Earl Bentz, founder and president of Triton Boat Company, whose support and friendship allowed me to become a full-time professional tournament bass fisherman and pursue the dream I love. A special thanks also goes to Ray Scott, founder of the Bass Anglers Sportsman Society, who first provided the playing field for those of us who enjoy competitive fishing so much. Among my fellow competitors, Charlie Ingram, Jimmy Houston, Bill Dance, and Rick Clunn have had a greater influence on my career than they'll ever know.

Writingwise, no one offered more encouragement than Patricia Parvin, who was always there to lean on when the computer screen seemed to turn blurry; and productionwise, a special thanks goes to my tireless editors at Falcon Publishing, Peggy O'Neill-McLeod and Patrick Straub, whose design talents turned a box of notes, pictures, and computer disks into a real book.

1
How It All Began

The road had been long and hard, and the rewards hardly outnumbered the disappointments. Still, I felt the time had come: I walked into the company office of Ken Younger, the President of Carolina Freight Company, and resigned from the only job I'd ever had.

"You're going full-time?" Ken asked.

"Yes," I answered, trying to muster stronger conviction in my voice than I actually felt inside. The year was 1986, and I was ending a 26-year career with the trucking company to embark on a totally new path.

I had decided to become a full-time professional tournament bass fisherman.

To my unending relief, Ken Younger encouraged me then and there. After all, I'd just completed a year of absence with his blessing to do nothing but fish tournaments, and I'd qualified for my fifth Bass Masters Classic that year. My sponsors had promised continued support, and my wife Pat had practically begged me to do it just so I'd stop worrying about it.

California angler Dave Gliebe helped bring flipping to the South. He and I often competed against each other in the American Bass Federation in the 1970s, and Dave still competes regularly in Western events.

"If it's what you really want to do, then I say you owe it to yourself to try, and I wish you nothing but success," said Younger as he shook my hand. "I've been reading about you in the papers and magazines. Just make sure I get to keep reading about you."

It would be easy to say that's how I became a bass pro, but it wouldn't be totally accurate. At the time I was 45 years old, and friends said I'd actually been preparing for my new job for 40 years. I really became a bass fisherman on Easter Sunday when I was five years old.

That day my father, Earl Eaker, took me fishing after church to a spot on the Catawba River, known as the Round Hole, not far from our home in Cherryville, North Carolina. He was a great live bait fisherman, so first we trapped a supply of minnows, then fished them on cane poles from the bank.

We caught five bass between 3 and 8 pounds. I caught the 3-pounder, or, as I think back on it, that fish caught me. From that day onward, all my fishing energy began to center around largemouth bass. Even when my father and I would go crappie fishing, I'd always put a larger-than-average minnow on a pole off to one side in hopes of catching a bass, and often I did. That's how I learned that bass like brush piles.

As I grew older, Dad took me fishing practically every weekend. Living in Cherryville as we did, there were plenty of nearby lakes to visit in both North and South Carolina, including Hickory, Johns River, Wylie, Wateree, and even Santee-Cooper's Marion and Moultrie. We spent a lot of time on the Catawba River itself, too, since Lake Norman had not yet been impounded.

I TRADED A SHOTGUN FOR MY FIRST BOAT

Every few years my father would make a wooden boat or two for some of his friends, and these were the first boats I used. My first boat was a wooden 17-foot flatbottom, although it wasn't one made by my father. I traded an old hammer-lock, double-barreled Winchester shotgun for it.

I'd actually traded a rod, reel, and box of lures for the shotgun some weeks earlier. The first time I shot the weapon it kicked me for a flip; I'd sneaked up on some ducks on the river and lined up three in a row. Then I cocked both hammers so I could make two quick shots. When I pulled the trigger, both barrels discharged, knocking me over backwards. I nailed all three ducks, but decided someone else could have more fun with that shotgun than I ever would.

The boat had high sides as well as an innovation: a livewell. I bought a Mercury Mark 28 outboard for it and a short sculling paddle to control the boat from the bow.

One day my uncle and some friends borrowed my boat for a fishing trip on Lake Wylie where I kept it. They didn't know much about boats, and out on the lake one of them opened the lid to the livewell, thinking it was a storage area. When he saw the water, he yelled that they were sinking, so they started bailing

Roland Martin, right, congratulates Bo Dowden, winner of the 1980 Bass Masters Classic at Thousand Islands, New York. That was my first Classic, and I finished twenty-first.

with a frying pan as fast as possible while my uncle got them back to shore. They'd never seen a livewell before!

In the mid-1960s I sold that little boat and bought my first real "bass boat," a Dixie Special with an 85-horsepower outboard and a trolling motor. No more hours of sitting on the bow casting with one hand and sculling with the other! With that boat I began to fish my first competitive tournaments, local events in which I did just well enough to keep fishing more of them.

In 1970 I entered my first major tournament, the North Carolina State Championship. It wasn't really a true state championship since there were no qualifying events and anyone could enter, but it was a big one-day tournament with dozens of top fishermen and more prize money than I'd ever competed for before. As the tournament began, I was so nervous I could hardly cast.

It was held on the lower end of Lake Norman, a portion of the new lake I had seldom fished. I was still too inexperienced to be confident about making the long run up the lake to the river where I usually fished, so I stayed fairly close to the launching area.

It was spring, and I fished a spinnerbait and jerkbait around some of the rock and grass points. The limit then was eight fish, and my eight weighed about 18 pounds, enough for fourth place and a check for $1,100. I didn't realize it then, but that first big tournament probably determined my future. I couldn't have been more excited if you'd handed me a million dollar check!

That tournament was conducted three more years, and I competed in each one, finishing ninth, 11th, and 21st. The same year of that final tournament, I organized the Cherryville Bassmasters and we joined the Bass Anglers Sportsman Society (B.A.S.S.) Federation. It was to be my home club for the next 13 years, and through it I learned many of the skills and techniques I use today.

This was competition in its purest form. We weren't fishing for money but rather for the competition and the club bragging rights that went with winning. I'd get so excited the night before one of our club events I wouldn't be able to sleep. I was actually more excited at those events than at the national B.A.S.S. tournaments I began fishing a few years later.

In 1973 and again in 1974, Northwest Bank in Charlotte sponsored two big tournaments on Lake Norman that drew between 250 and 300 anglers each year. I won both events, and with each win came checks of around $3,000 plus additional equipment.

The following year, a national bass fishing organization, the American Bass Federation (ABF), conducted one of their tournaments on Lake Norman. I was a member of ABF so I entered, and I won, boating a little over 28 pounds in two days.

MY FIRST FLORIDA TOURNAMENT

That win gave me a free entry into the ABF World Championship that autumn on Florida's Lake Kissimmee. I'd never been to Florida before and when I first looked at the lake, all my fears from that first North Carolina State Championship in 1970 returned. Not only was I competing against some of the country's best fishermen like Roland Martin and Tom Mann, but the only thing I could see across that lake was grass.

It all looked the same to me. I was afraid to go very far because I was certain I'd get lost! This was also my first three-day tournament, so the first day I only went about five miles away and managed to scratch up two bass. The next day, on the advice of some other anglers, I moved out about 12 or 14 miles. I found a grassy shoreline and started throwing a spinnerbait.

I'd covered perhaps 500 yards of shoreline without a strike and was feeling pretty discouraged when a 2-pound bass finally hit. I couldn't figure out why on earth that bass was where it was until I looked around me. Suddenly I saw it: the top of the grass where the bass came from was about six inches lower than everywhere else I'd been fishing!

That was my first experience in seeing how subtle some bass patterns can be, especially where both vegetation and depth are factors. From that point on, I concentrated on the slightly deeper water and probably lost enough big bass to have won the tournament. I did land a 9-14 lunker that won big bass honors, and finished ninth overall with 38 pounds.

My next ABF tournament was on Lake Murray in South Carolina, and there Roland Martin asked me to join him in giving a seminar that week in Knoxville,

One of my proudest days as a bass fisherman and as a tournament professional came when I fished with United States President George Bush and we won Ray Scott's second Pintlala "Eagles of Angling" tournament. My close friend Charlie Ingram, right, helps hold our trophy.

Tennessee. It meant losing one day of practice, and I'd never been on an airplane before, and I'd certainly never given a seminar, but I went anyway.

I couldn't believe it when I walked out on the stage, because there must have been 3,000 people in the audience. Somehow I survived, just talking as I normally do about how to fish crankbaits.

What made it even more difficult was knowing that two of the nation's best crankbait fishermen were sitting in the audience. They were Mike Estep, who was probably the first to put rattles in wood crankbaits; and Fred Young, the man who created the famous Big O lure that really made crankbait fishing so popular. After I finished speaking, I had the honor of introducing them to the audience, which was really a thrill for me.

We drove all the way back to Lake Murray that night, just in time to practice the next day. I found some really good fish and led the tournament the first two days, then lost the final day to finish second.

I fished all the remaining ABF events that year and earned a check in each one. I missed winning the Angler of the Year title by about 3 pounds. My excitement knew no bounds at my quick success thus far, so I quickly entered all the ABF tournaments for the following year, and in the first tournament of the new season, I won at Lake Seminole, beating California angler Dave Gliebe by just 3 ounces.

KEEP FISHING UNTIL THE VERY END

In that tournament I learned just how important it is to keep fishing as hard as you can until the very end. With five minutes left to go and me about four minutes from the weigh-in, I caught a 1½-pound bass. That's the fish that won for me.

Throughout that season, Gliebe and I had a wonderful race for Angler of the Year. Dave, of course, is the angler who brought the technique of flipping to the South, and he was a master at using it to catch fish the rest of us missed or couldn't reach. It was anybody's title as we went into the final tournament of the year at Lake Cumberland, a deep, clear, and rocky impoundment in Kentucky.

It was a tough tournament for me, as I could only manage 4 or 5 pounds a day, but it was tougher for Gliebe, and I won the Angler of the Year title. The next year I finished second, then third the following year, and in my last season with ABF, fifth.

In 1980 I began fishing the B.A.S.S. Tournament Trail, and in my very first tournament with them I finished third. I qualified for my first Bass Masters Classic that year, finishing 21st at Thousand Islands, New York. I made the Classic again in both 1981 and 1982, then missed it in both 1983 and 1984.

By now my tournament schedule was outrunning my vacation time from Carolina Freight. In fact, I had to miss B.A.S.S. events in 1983 and 1984 because I couldn't get anyone to take my shift at work. I was a supervisor on the loading dock and had to develop a schedule of working 13 hours a day, three days a week, then paying others to work for me at $200 per day. I'd been doing this for 10 years but it really wasn't working, even though Carolina Freight allowed me to do it. That's when I went back to Ken and submitted my resignation.

NO REGRETS

In the years since, my career has had as many moments of excitement and let-downs as anyone else. Professional bass fishing is that type of sport. Overall, however, I've never had any regrets about the decision I made that day in 1986.

After all, how many people have a career doing exactly what they really and truly love to do? Not as many as we'd all like to believe, unfortunately. Fishing has allowed me not only to travel throughout the United States but also to foreign countries, where I've discovered fishing really is a common language, even though the species, equipment, and techniques may be different.

I've been privileged to spend a day in the boat fishing with the president of the United States and even managed to get a fish hook out of his hand. My reward for that? An unforgettable personalized tour of the Air Force One, but even more importantly, a friendship that continues today, years after the event.

I've seen the sport of bass fishing grow tremendously since my days with my father in that wooden boat, but the thrill of catching bass today compared to 40 years ago hasn't changed a bit. I still love every second of it.

2

A Bass Is a Bass Is a Bass

There is no question that the more you know and understand about bass and their behavior, the more success you'll have catching them. The only problem is, just about the time you think you really do have them figured out, the fish will do something totally out of the ordinary and put you back at square one! It happens all the time.

Still, it's worth your time and effort to learn all you can about the bass, not only because it does have some fairly predictable habits but also because of those unpredictable times. The more you know about your quarry, the better your chances for figuring out what it's going to take to catch them.

First, don't think of bass as intelligent. We all tend to think of fish, as well as wildlife like deer and wild turkey, in human terms of intelligence and reasoning

Largemouth bass live in 49 of the 50 states, and several foreign countries. Regardless of where they live, they share the same requirements, and the more you learn about them the better angler you'll become.

power, and that's a mistake. When you do think like this, you're helping to defeat yourself.

Bass act and react by instinct. For them, basically everything they do is for survival, and over millions of years, the fish have evolved some amazingly efficient survival instincts. Understanding these survival instincts is what allows us to overcome them so we feel that wonderful pull at the end of our line.

To me, one of the most amazing survival mechanisms the bass has is its ability to detect sound vibrations in the water. These vibrations tell the fish where bait is located as well as where danger lurks.

LATERAL LINES PICK UP VIBRATIONS

The lateral line on the bass picks up most of these sound vibrations. This is the dark line running along each side of the bass from just behind the gills to the tail; it's a series of nerve endings that tells the fish how far away something is, how big it is, and how fast it's moving.

Somehow, the lateral line also tells the bass whether the vibrations are normal or abnormal. The bass probably can't specifically identify the source of the vibrations as a minnow or crayfish but it seems to be able to tell if it isn't moving the way it should.

How does knowing this help us as bass fishermen? It tells us that making unusual retrieves, such as stop-and-go or rise-and-fall, are often more effective than a straight back-to-the-boat retrieve. My friend Ken Cook proved this when he won the 1991 Bass Masters Classic at Chesapeake Bay by fluttering his spinnerbait down into clumps of vegetation.

That means the bass has at least two constantly working mechanisms that not only tell it where food is but also where danger may be. Bouncing your boat off stumps, or even dropping tackle boxes in the boat also send vibrations to the fish.

So does your trolling motor, especially when you continually turn it on, then off, then on again. I have found when I'm fishing very tight to cover that it is much better to simply leave the trolling motor on low power the entire time. It's as if the bass become accustomed to it and simply accept the noise as part of their environment.

USE YOUR DEPTHFINDER WITH CARE

Bass can even detect the sonar signals from your depthfinder, not only in shallow water, but also at deeper depths. Several guides have told me about watching schools of bass at 20 feet move as they sat above them watching on a depthfinder. Thus, when I'm fishing shallow water, I turn my depthfinder off once I know the bottom configuration.

I also believe bass probably see better than we sometimes think they do, and I base this not only on my experiences as an angler but also as a fish owner. For three years I kept a largemouth bass in a 120-gallon aquarium in my home. My daughter caught the fish when it was about 5 inches long, and I kept it until it weighed nearly 4½ pounds.

The aquarium was in my living room where I could see the bass while I read the newspaper or watched television. Most of the time, I noticed, the bass watched me intently while I was doing this, its nose pressed right against the aquarium glass. All I had to do to make the bass dart to the back of the aquarium was tap my foot on the floor. Not get up, not raise my hand, but simply tap my foot. The fish saw the movement as well as felt the vibrations. With movement as insignificant as this, there's no doubt in my mind bass know about our presence in their territory long before we ever know of theirs. They also know about our lures the instant they touch the water.

Another characteristic I noticed about my aquarium fish that has helped me in my fishing is the way it fed. The bass usually sucked in its food from several inches away, often from at least a foot away.

That tells me to set the hook when I first feel the slightest "tic" or "tap" on my worm or jig, or the lure's going to be spit out. Don't wait for a repeat "tap." This makes using longer rods more efficient because the arc of your hook-set takes up the slack line you normally have.

Are you beginning to see why knowing as much as you can about the habits of bass will help you catch more of them?

EXPELLED SCALES

Whenever my aquarium bass ate a minnow, which was often, it not only sucked in the fish, it literally scaled it. Seconds after inhaling the minnow, it blew out scales, aquarium gravel, and water through its gills. Other fish in the aquarium immediately became aroused by these scales and seemed to want to get in on the feeding activity.

That's when I began thinking about gold-and-silver flake skirts for my spinnerbaits. In clear water, I wondered, would bass think the skirts were expelled scales from a feeding bass?

I had some of the skirts made by RM Engineering, and today I can honestly say they seem to make a difference. Since I've started using them, I have caught more bass in clear water than ever before, and other anglers have noticed similar results. That's why many spinnerbait manufacturers have developed new skirt, blade, and head combinations. With these changes, spinnerbaits are more attractive to bass than we ever imagined.

BASS ARE ADAPTABLE

It's important to understand just how adaptable bass really are. They live in every state except Alaska, in big lakes, small ponds, fast-moving rivers, slow creeks,

Always look at the big picture of what the bass has available in the form of food and habitat. Isolated cover like this duck blind often holds fish because it may be the only cover available.

swamps, and of course, aquariums like the one I had. The survival instincts that rule the lifestyle of bass allow them to not only live but also thrive in each of these different environments.

At the same time, it's important to understand that a bass is a bass is a bass wherever it does happen to live. There are some basic requirements and habits that do not change, no matter where the fish lives. This is why tournament pros can use the same general tactics and equipment on any lake and still catch them. For example, we know bass are basically shallow water residents; the majority of tournaments are won fishing water no deeper than about eight feet. We also know bass prefer to stay around cover such as stumps, trees, and vegetation.

How do we catch such heavy stringers of bass from a monstrous body of water like Lake Ontario, for instance? We don't even think about the deep, wide-open parts of the lake. Instead, we concentrate on shallow, rock-filled bays and coves and fish spinnerbaits just like we would on Toledo Bend or Lake Seminole. We're simply keying on the basics.

These two constants, shallow water and cover, as much as anything else, should form the foundation of your fishing knowledge. They will not, however, be enough. There are many different variables that dictate just where bass will be in shallow water and how they act there. Some of these variables include water temperature, oxygen content of the water, water clarity, the presence or absence of baitfish, the pH of the water, and, as we're learning more and more, angling pressure. And there are other variables too.

BASS ARE THE SAME, BUT LAKES ARE DIFFERENT

What you must keep in mind throughout your fishing is while a bass is a bass is a bass, not every lake is a lake is a lake. By this I mean the dynamics of each lake are different and you have to adjust to them. While it is important to understand how some of the above variables affect bass behavior generally, you must always look at the variables in the context of the particular lake you're fishing.

Those bays on Lake Ontario, for example, hold bass not only because they're shallow and filled with cover, but because other conditions, such as the presence of baitfish, the water's oxygen content, and water clarity, are also agreeable to the bass.

Not all the bays and coves on Lake Ontario hold concentrations of bass, and not all the bass in Lake Ontario are in the coves. See what I'm getting at here? Whenever you're on the water trying to figure out where the fish are or what's going to make them bite, you have to look at the entire picture of what's available for the bass in the way of habitat and the other variables. They're all interrelated in a particular way on that particular lake at that particular time.

Let me give you another example of bass behavior to help explain what I mean. During the 1987 Bass Masters Classic on the Ohio River out of Louisville, Kentucky, we were fishing a stretch of the river where the nearest tributary creeks were more than 100 river miles away. There was very little shoreline cover along the river itself, so each day of competition I raced 125 miles downriver to fish one particular creek.

The fishing was tough, and I eventually finished third overall with just over 12 pounds of bass. George Cochran won with 15 pounds, 5 ounces of bass—all caught along a small grass bed practically within casting distance of the ramp where we launched!

I knew about the grass bed, and because it was basically the only real cover along the river, I knew it would hold bass. I also knew the creeks would hold bass, which they did. I was willing to make the long boat trips and gamble that I could catch more bass than George, but you might not be so willing. Remember the basics. We both caught bass, in totally different places, but both spots were shallow and had cover available.

KEEP AN OPEN MIND

As you continue to learn about bass, keep an open mind about what you read compared to what you experience. Bass fishing is filled with theories from the earliest days of the sport that many of us have considered to be irrefutable until recent years. At the same time, one experience on the water does not mean bass will act that way every day.

We do know bass move both vertically and horizontally to find conditions better suited for a particular activity like spring spawning, or simply more agreeable for their survival requirements, such as fall feeding in creeks. Often, however, these movements are not as great as once thought; we continually catch bass within 300 to 400 yards of a primary spawning area, and in some creeks we catch them year-round.

Most of us now believe if bass have a suitable area, such as a creek with available cover and a reasonable channel that offers some depth, then bass will remain in that creek throughout the year. I just don't believe the bass I caught in that creek in the 1987 Classic would leave and swim 125 miles to be around Cochran's grass bed, or that the fish there would swim all the way downriver just to be in my creek. There is no reason for them to do it.

BASS MOVE

This is not to say bass don't move at all, because they do. Anglers form nearly all their fish-catching strategy on four very broad, basic seasonal movements or "patterns" bass make. In spring, bass come shallow to spawn, moving onto wide, hard bottom flats, coves, and points. This takes place from January to June, depending on the region of the country.

After spawning, the bass move to deeper structures like creek channels, ledges, or underwater humps where they remain for the summer. In fall the bass move

If you think in terms of shallow water and heavy cover, you'll usually be close to bass. In shallow water like this, lure presentation becomes extremely important, but this is the type of water most pros prefer.

from these structures to creeks where they feed heavily on shad and other baitfish. In winter the bass leave the creeks and relocate on deeper structures once more.

You should certainly keep these movements in mind whenever you fish, but at the same time remember that variables can and will alter the schedule. An abnormally warm winter will send bass shallow early; a very cold winter will keep them deeper longer. On Choke Canyon Lake in Texas, the cover itself—acres of flooded timber—is a variable; many bass actually spawn on big tree limbs rather than in shallow flats.

We'll discuss more about finding bass in the next chapter, but for now the question is how much time should you spend examining all the variables in a particular area?

The answer, of course, is as much time as it takes to find the fish. In tournament competition this is called "defining a pattern," and sometimes it actually takes several days to accomplish. Every pro, myself included, has also fished entire tournaments without defining anything!

If the habitat is good but you're not catching bass, then you have to begin checking the variables one by one—and this is where your overall knowledge of bass behavior becomes so important.

For example, check the water temperature—it only takes a second with your electronics. Warm water holds less oxygen than cold water so when the water temperature rises above about 80 degrees the bass usually move deeper. Have you been fishing too shallow for the conditions?

I can't tell you a specific order in which to check the variables I listed earlier. All I want you to do is learn as much as you can about bass so you begin to check these variables automatically without even thinking about them.

You'll begin to notice the water temperature; you'll see that baitfish flicking the surface 20 yards ahead of your boat; you'll automatically register water color as your lure disappears within two feet of the surface.

There is no substitute for time on the water. Many of the top bass tournament anglers today were, or still are, professional guides who spend thousands of hours annually in pursuit of bass for their clients.

In the process, they gain incredible amounts of knowledge about bass habits so that when they begin practicing for a tournament on some strange lake, they remember the basics and they know how to study the big picture.

A good lake map with a contour interval of five feet will show the kind of depth detail needed to locate places bass might be. It will also show cover like stumps and timber.

3

TRICKS FOR FINDING BASS

Without doubt, the biggest problem bass anglers face each time they go to a lake is finding the fish. Looking out over 100,000 acres of water that usually stretches to the horizon and beyond, and realizing the myriad places bass might be, can be pretty intimidating, even to an experienced fisherman.

The problem gets worse if you've never been on the lake before, and if you only have a limited amount of time to find the fish—conditions tournament anglers face regularly. That's why the pros have developed and refined several techniques for finding bass quickly on virtually any lake we fish.

The secret is not to fish an entire lake, but only a small part of it. By small, I mean a single large tributary, or perhaps a two- to three-mile section that might include several small tributaries. The term used to describe this concept is "confidence area fishing," and the more skill you develop in using this technique, the more bass you'll catch.

The primary criteria for any confidence area are that it include a variety of cover, structure, and depth options for bass to use. I want points and coves, shallow shoreline brush, ditches, and a well-defined creek channel. Grass or other vegetation is wonderful, and so is dingy water. Riprap, piers and boathouses, and underwater roadbeds are all things I'd like the area to have too.

In short, I want the confidence area to be a miniature version of the lake itself, offering bass all the same cover and structure options they have in the big water. When bass have all these choices, I'm not sure they ever leave, and that's what makes the entire confidence area technique so important.

You can fish a confidence area in a few hours and determine one or more patterns if you do it properly; out on the main lake it could take you days to learn the same things.

START WITH A GOOD MAP

When I'm looking for a confidence area, I start by studying a good lake map. I want a map with a contour interval of five feet if I can find one because this is the kind of detail that helps pinpoint bass. When the contour interval is 20 feet (each wavy line on the map equals a depth variation of 20 feet) you're not going to learn very much.

A good lake map will show cover, such as stump fields and flooded timber, and it will also show you something else many anglers overlook: the actual shoreline configuration. The best shorelines on any lake are those with the most irregularities, such as little points, indentations, and coves. These give baitfish—and bass— more places to use.

Some basic rules generally hold true for confidence areas. First, remember the upper reaches of a lake will be shallower and generally more off-colored. If you're fishing a clear lake, this might be where your confidence area should be.

Second, vegetation like milfoil and hydrilla will attract and hold bass year-round in some lakes, and it is always worth looking for, regardless of which end of a lake it may be growing. If a lake has an abundance of vegetation, you will usually need to consider a second attractive feature within the grass itself, such as stumps, creek channels, or points, when looking for a confidence area.

Third, always consider the history of the lake you're fishing. This will give you an idea of what to expect in the way of fish numbers and the size of the fish. For example, if the lake has a history of producing few fish, then you may decide on a confidence area that offers the heaviest cover available.

On the other hand, if the lake has a history of producing a lot of quality fish, then you should definitely look at the areas where these fish are normally caught. On Sam Rayburn Reservoir in Texas, for instance, a number of well-known areas produce bass consistently, and I made one of them, the Black Forest, my confidence area when I won the 1994 Texas Bassmaster Invitational.

The most common confidence areas are major tributaries, but not all of them. Much depends on the body of water you're fishing. Because I am primarily a shallow water fisherman and spend much of my time with a spinnerbait, my confidence areas often became the far upper reaches of a lake where it's actually more of a river. I choose these places because they offer the two primary ingredients I need for a spinnerbait: dingy water and shallow cover.

FISH TO YOUR STRENGTH

As tournament bass fishing becomes more competitive and the overall fishing more difficult, I think it's important to at least consider choosing a confidence area that allows you to fish the way you want to fish. That is, if you want to flip a jig or worm, then your area should have plenty of jig/worm water and cover. The same is true for crankbaits, topwaters, or any other lure or technique.

This is called fishing to your strength, and the advantage it offers is one of confidence. You will naturally perform better if you are really familiar with a lure or technique and enjoy it.

Some pros choose tiny, practically inaccessible creeks that other anglers never even notice for their confidence areas. Their reasoning is that these places have not received much fishing pressure so the bass might not only be fairly numerous but also more willing to bite. Sometimes these places are so small they're hardly even noticeable on a map; other times they're simply too far from the launching area for most anglers to bother visiting. Traditionally, they have shallow water and abundant cover and are best suited to flipping and pitching, although I've found some where a spinnerbait worked just fine.

Still another confidence area choice is to locate a big spawning flat, either on the main lake or in a major tributary creek (your map will show you this), and simply work out from it to the nearest cover or channel. Crisscross or zigzag out from the shallow water watching your depthfinder for a breakline on a ditch or creek channel. Bass really don't move that far from their spawning grounds if they don't need to.

If you can't find a breakline as you move out from a spawning flat, look instead for cover. This can be the edge of an underwater grassline, a row of standing timber, or a field of stumps. Bass are object-oriented and will hold by these places not only as they move into and out of a spawning area, but also for much of the rest of the year if other conditions are favorable.

Whether you choose a major tributary, a tiny hidden creek, the upper river portion of your lake, or a huge spawning flat as your confidence area, you can fine-tune the process further by dividing the entire lake and its tributaries into sections. Basically, this shows you at a glance where shallow, intermediate, and deep water are. You choose your water type according to the season of the year.

MARKING YOUR MAP

A lot of experienced pros I know do this mentally, but Rick Clunn showed me how to do it with a ruler and pen. If you do it this way, you'll be amazed at the perspective it will give you. If you know the basic activity bass will be following at the time of year you're fishing, marking a map like this will show where that activity is most likely to take place.

Using your map and ruler, draw a line straight across the lake about a third of the way up from the dam. This will be section one. Now, draw a second line about two-thirds of the way up from the dam. Everything below this line—the midsection of the lake—is section two, while everything above it is section three. You can even make a section four if you like, marking the far upper end of the lake at the point it becomes a river. Mark all the major tributary creeks the same way.

What you've just done is isolate (or eliminate) all the lake's deep water as well as its clear water. The deep water of section one will usually be clearer, it will be the last to warm in spring and have the latest spawn. By contrast, section three (and section four, if you marked it) will show you shallow water that will almost certainly have more "color" to it; this is the water that will warm the fastest in spring and cool the quickest in fall.

MATCH THE SEASONAL PATTERNS

Now all you have to do is match seasonal bass patterns (which we discussed in chapter 2) to the lake sections. For example, in the fall, one major bass pattern

You may decide to make your confidence area the back of a tributary where the water is often dingy. Here spinnerbait pro Paul Chapple of Alabama tries a creek on Lay Lake.

is fishing the backs of creeks where bass are feeding, so you know you can concentrate on section three. Look at all the places you have a section three, compare them, and choose the one that gives you the most fishing options.

Even though you may be completely familiar with seasonal patterns of bass and know exactly where you plan to fish, marking a lake map like this helps you form an overall game plan. It is especially helpful on lakes you haven't been on before because it helps you organize your thoughts so you can create a fishing strategy.

Your choice of a confidence area has effectively eliminated the majority of the lake, but you're still faced with the same problem of actually locating the bass. Although now you're fishing a much smaller area, you still have to remain organized and focused, and you do this by eliminating all those options we talked about earlier, one at a time.

Look over your area and pick the easiest option to eliminate first. It could be boathouses, points, or even a stretch of riprap. Each of these could be a place to start, but remember you can't eliminate points by simply fishing one of them. You have to work several of them; dissect them with a crankbait or Carolina rig at various depths and make sure the bass are not on them before you move to the new option, such as the boathouses.

When I go through this sequence, I keep telling myself even though I may not be catching any bass, I'm getting closer to them. Learning where bass are not is every bit as important as learning where they are, and eliminating options is how you do it.

Earlier in this chapter I mentioned fishing to your strength, such as looking for water or conditions that allow you to use your favorite lure or technique. This is when you really want to do it. For me, the first thing I'm going to do in my confidence area is head to shallow brush in off-colored water where I can use a spinnerbait. If I catch bass doing this, not only is my confidence level going to soar, I have also given myself more time to locate additional bass with a secondary or backup pattern.

One of the things you'll need to be aware of in your confidence area is something we call "timing." This is recognizing what bass are doing at a specific time, and believe me, it can be frustrating. The way you solve this part of the bass location puzzle is by visiting certain spots several times during a day if necessary.

For example, let's say your confidence area has several very good looking points in it, each with cover and depth changes. It's the time of year when bass should be on the points, but nothing you throw gets so much as a nibble.

TRY THE NEXT OPTION

Don't give up. Go to the next option, such as the boathouses, and fish them as carefully as you did the points. Then after an hour or two, check one of the points again. Something may have changed and caused the bass to move up on the points while you were fishing the boathouses. It could be cloud cover that built up, a wind that began to ripple the surface, or perhaps engineers starting to release water at the dam and creating a current. There are hundreds of reasons bass might move up or back or out or down, and you need to be aware of some of them. Remember the question of variables we discussed in chapter 2? These are some of them.

Among the most important variables that are easily noticeable and which seem to have the strongest effect on bass are weather, water temperature, the presence of baitfish, and current. None of these factors consistently influences bass the same way on every lake, so what you as a fisherman must do in your confidence area is to try to be aware of variables like this as you fish. Is the wind blowing or not? Is it bright and sunny, or is there cloud cover? Was it a cold morning but warming up by midafternoon? Did you see any baitfish activity?

Experienced pros have learned to observe these things without consciously thinking about them. As I said before, this comes from spending time on the water, and it'll come to you if you fish long enough. There is no substitute for time on the water.

One key that will help is noticing the activity of birds, squirrels, cattle, or other wildlife along the shore where you're fishing. When they're active, bass are usually active too, but when they aren't, you can pretty well bet the fishing will be slow.

Understanding and recognizing these factors will help keep you from becoming discouraged when the bass aren't as active as you'd like them to be. Keep in mind that by fishing a small confidence area you're much closer to the bass than you would be on the open lake, and eventually you are going to find them.

4

Five Quick Patterns to Remember

Several years ago RM Engineering sent me some new spinnerbait skirts to evaluate, and because I only had a single afternoon available for testing, I decided to spend it on Lake Wylie, an excellent Catawba River impoundment I have fished often.

I had not been on Wylie for months prior to the test, however, so without any time to spare looking for bass, I headed straight into Little Allison Creek and began fishing the boat docks, making parallel casts along the pilings. Five hours later I decided RM had produced an excellent lure color, as I had caught eight bass weighing 48 pounds.

What made me head straight to the boat docks, rather than creek channels, points, or anywhere else?

Much of my decision was based on my previous experience on Lake Wylie and other lakes over the years where I had caught bass around boat docks before. Another reason is that no matter where you fish, a bass is still a bass. There are certain conditions the fish generally relate to if they're available, and you need to keep these in mind.

MY FIVE FAVORITE LOCATIONS

I have five favorite places I like to look for bass, especially when I'm either in a hurry as I was at Lake Wylie, or when nothing else I try seems to work. These five places include boat docks; riprap; points; vegetation, like hydrilla, milfoil, or moss; and main lake pockets.

These places do not necessarily produce the largest bass (although my Lake Wylie stringer included one fish over 8 pounds and another over 7) or the most. In some cases, you could almost label them "last ditch tactics," because they aren't your primary pattern choices for the water you're fishing. Overall, however, one or more of these places will nearly always be present on almost every lake you fish, and it will hold some fish.

1. Boat Docks

Although they are never the most glamorous places to fish, boat docks can attract surprisingly high concentrations of bass. They're especially worth trying during

Boat docks are seldom glamorous places to fish, but they usually hold a few bass because they often provide shade and cover close to deeper water as well as structure for bass to relate to.

the spring when bass move shallow to spawn, but they can be just as productive in the summer, fall, and dead of winter.

One reason is because many boat docks offer the magic combination of shallow water adjacent to deep water. This is why boat docks located on the points leading into a creek or cove are normally the most productive. Migrating fish coming into the coves stop at these docks first. A deep/shallow combination gives bass the opportunity to move vertically into a feeding zone or deeper into a safety zone without having to make a long horizontal movement.

Another reason boat docks produce good fishing is because owners frequently put brush under them to attract fish. Your key that brush may be under the surface is the presence of rod holders and/or lights around the edge of the dock. The brush attracts minnows which attract crappie and bass.

In addition, docks also offer shade and cover, which makes them good places to fish on lakes that have a lot of pleasure boat and ski traffic, and they're probably the best places to fish on lakes that have little other shoreline cover.

My favorite lure for boat dock fishing is a ½-ounce jig, but I'll also use spinnerbaits and crankbaits, and even topwater buzz baits and chuggers. Crankbaits are effective for finding the brush piles under the surface, but you can also do this with a jig.

2. Riprap

Riprap is the rock used around bridges and causeways to add support to the structure and help prevent erosion. At times they're magnets for bass because the rocks offer hiding places for crawfish and other creatures bass eat, and also because algae grow on the rocks to provide food for minnows.

Nearly all riprap will also offer shallow water close to deep water, especially the riprap around bridges. As with boat docks, the bass are able to move vertically rather than horizontally.

There are numerous ways to fish riprap but one of my favorite techniques is to parallel cast a crankbait, worm, or jig along the rocks, probing different depths until I locate fish. I usually start on any little point or bend the riprap makes.

Another way to fish riprap is by casting directly into it and working your lure down the slope. This can be extremely productive with a big blade spinnerbait if you let it flutter and fall in a series of hops.

Don't hesitate to use a buzz bait around the riprap either, even in the heat of the day. Buzz baits are well known for being able to "call" or attract bass up from deeper water, and I've caught some huge fish around riprap by clinking a buzz bait slowly along the edge of the rocks.

In spring, bass may spawn around the rocks, so consider pitching a jig around the edges of the riprap where the rocks end. In winter, riprap usually provides better afternoon fishing because the sun has warmed the rocks, which in turn might warm the water around them. Bass rise from the deeper water to suspend close to the riprap.

3. Points

Entering the final day of the 1994 Oklahoma Bassmaster Invitational on Lake Texoma, I stood in thirty-first place, and when the day dawned stormy and blustery, I had to change patterns and places entirely because the weather was so bad. Instead of crossing the open water to reach Mill Creek where I'd been working a crankbait, I headed up the Washita River arm and began crankbaiting Cumberland Point. There, at least, I could control my boat in the wind. I found the bass on the very tip of the point and caught a limit from one spot; my stringer weighed 11-8 and jumped me into second place for the tournament.

Of all places you can choose to fish on a major impoundment, points are among the most dependable. In early spring, bass usually move to the points first before continuing to spawning areas. In summer, bass move up and down points as water levels and temperatures dictate; and in winter, points provide quick access to deeper water.

Even when water levels are changing or when a current is present, bass gravitate toward points. The familiar saying, "Points point out bass in falling water" is true; as water levels drop, the fish simply move farther and farther down the point.

I remember watching bass on my depthfinder as they moved from a deep channel where they'd been all morning up on a point where they began feeding

Points can be dependable places to find bass, especially during changing water conditions. I usually fish the deeper water first with either a crankbait or Carolina-rigged lizard, and gradually move shallow.

once the Corps of Engineers began pulling water through a dam in early afternoon. We'd caught one bass during the morning, even though we could clearly see them, but within 30 minutes after the fish moved up on the point we had nearly two limits, including a nice 7-pounder.

There are numerous ways to fish points, but two of the best are to begin by using either a Carolina-rigged lizard or a deep-diving crankbait. These lures let you cover a lot of water in a hurry, and they'll also bring reaction strikes if the bass are even remotely active.

Work from deep to shallow

I like to start in the deeper water and gradually work up the point into shallow water. That way, if bass are shallow, I won't be spooking them with the boat. I pick a spot and fan-cast the point, covering a wide angle of water. Then I move to a new spot and do the same thing.

If any current is present, you'll probably have better success by positioning yourself on the downstream side of the point and casting across it so your retrieve comes with that current. Bass will often line up on the back side of a point so they can intercept any food being washed across in front of them. Frequently, your best spot will be around the tip too, where the point begins to drop into deeper water.

Lure-wise, crankbaits are probably the best choice for fishing points when current is flowing, but your choice really must depend on the cover available and the water temperature. Crankbaits work well in the spring, summer, and fall, but in winter you may need to change to a jig.

Some of the best points are those formed at the mouths of tributary streams. These points extend much farther out underwater than many anglers realize, and frequently the best fishing spots are where that point intersects that main river channel. If stumps, rocks, or other cover is available on these points, they'll become a magnet for fish.

4. Vegetation

Many of my friends in professional fishing tell me if a lake has any type of vegetation in it, that's the first place they're going to look for fish, and I usually agree with them. Vegetation, such as hydrilla, milfoil, coontail moss, or any of the other varieties, is generally considered perfect bass habitat because it provides shade, cover, and food. If you look at any of the top bass lakes in America today, the one common denominator they have is abundant vegetation.

In many instances, the best way to fish vegetation is to fish the edges, either the outside edge where the water becomes deeper, or the inside edge where it is more shallow. In early spring, when bass want to spawn, the inside edge may be better, as bass stage there before making the final move into the shallows to nest; at other times of the year, the outside edges are often better.

Vegetation is always a good place to look for bass, regardless of what type of vegetation it may be. Here two anglers land a nice bass around the reeds in Lake Seminole.

Whenever I want to catch a really big stringer of bass, I use a ½- or ¾-ounce spinnerbait and work it along the outside edge. We're talking underwater vegetation now that may still be two to three feet below the surface; you may be able to see the edge, or you may have to follow it with your depthfinder, but the key is to cast over the vegetation, let your lure sink down to the top of it, then retrieve so the spinnerbait falls over the drop. This is typically known as "slow-rolling" because the retrieve is fairly slow.

Following vegetation lines with your depthfinder is not difficult once you learn to recognize what you're seeing, and most of today's quality sonar units make the task even easier. What you really try to concentrate on are indentions or points that break up the otherwise straight line of the grass; these are frequently where you find fish.

One thing many anglers do when fishing grass like this is to keep a marker buoy ready to drop overboard when they catch a bass because the fish often concentrate in schools along the edges.

Crankbaits can also be used over the top of the vegetation; one of the favorite spring patterns on grass-filled Sam Rayburn and other similar lakes is reeling a lipless crankbait right over the top of the submerged grass as fast as you can turn

Bill Dance and Loren Hill enjoy some smallmouth success in a rocky cove in Pickwick Lake. Look for main lake pockets with rock or gravel bottoms and nearby deep water.

the reel handle. Bass not only hold in the grass, but they spawn in it too, and this is one way to get reaction strikes.

Later in the summer when the vegetation has grown to the surface, I like to use a ³⁄₁₆- or ¼-ounce spinnerbait and simply fish over the top of the green stuff. I try to guide the spinnerbait to any potholes and openings where I can swim the lure like a small minnow.

Other anglers in the South fish plastic frogs across the surface of the matted vegetation, and there is hardly a more exciting way to catch bass. This is known as "rat fishing," and while it may not produce a lot of strikes in a day, the strikes it does bring are frequently from huge bass that literally explode through the vegetation to hit the lure.

Still another way to fish matted vegetation is to work the openings with jigs or plastic worms, pitching into them and then letting the lure sink into the open water below. This is a popular technique on Toledo Bend and other lakes where the vegetation is thick in the summer. It's only thick on the surface, however, for underneath the water is open where it provides excellent cover for the bass.

5. Main Lake Pockets

By main lake pockets, I'm describing flats and coves off the main lake where bass come in the spring to spawn and in the summer and fall to feed. When you're looking for bass in places like this, the primary ingredients are a hard sand or gravel bottom (bass don't like silty bottoms) and deep water nearby.

These spots are easily recognized on a lake map because the bottom contour of the pocket itself will be fairly flat. If the pocket has a ditch or small creek flowing through it, so much the better. Bass will use this channel as a migration route to and from the deeper water.

In the summer I like to fish these pockets with a topwater chugger, and if you try it, be in position before the sun rises. Once the sun clears the horizon, the topwater bite disappears very quickly. After that you'll need to change to a Carolina rig or possibly a crankbait.

At other times of the year, crankbaits and spinnerbaits may be your top lure choices, especially if the pocket has abundant cover. These are good places to catch big bass in both the early spring and fall, and numbers of fish the rest of the year.

5

WATER TEMPERATURE AND BASS BEHAVIOR

Of all the external factors that change bass behavior and their willingness to hit our lures, I believe water temperature is one of the most critical. Even though scientists are actively conducting research in this field, it doesn't take serious bass fishermen long to experience how a change in water temperature will cause a bass to act differently.

For example, I know my win in the 1994 Texas Bassmaster Invitational at Sam Rayburn was influenced by a sudden drop in water temperature caused by a massive cold front. The bass were in shallow water cover preparing to spawn, but when the front hit and water temperatures dropped 10 degrees, the bass moved nearly 50 yards back to deeper water where the temperature was more stable.

Because I always pay attention to the weather, I knew the storm was coming and located the area I felt the bass would move to before they got there; after the front hit, that's exactly where I caught them.

Water temperature changes, especially sudden changes, will cause bass to relocate, or certainly become less active (sometimes almost totally inactive) in a matter of hours. This is because bass are cold-blooded. Their body and blood temperature are basically the same as the water around them. Their body temperature, and thus the water temperature, controls their metabolism—their level of feeding and food digestion. Largemouth bass have a comfort zone of approximately 60 to 75 degrees during which they are the most active. This is when a largemouth's metabolism uses up energy the quickest, meaning it will feed (or strike our lures) most often.

Naturally other factors can and do influence bass behavior, even if the water temperature is an optimum 72 degrees, but let's not worry about those factors now. Let's concentrate solely on water temperature.

Bass, of course, live, feed, and survive in water both colder and warmer than their comfort range. I have caught fish in winter when the water temperature registered in the low 40s, and I have also caught bass in Florida in 85-degree water.

METABOLISM SLOWS IN COLD WATER

In colder water, the metabolism of largemouth continues to slow until it needs only a minnow or two every week to survive. Larry Barnes, a Lake Fork, Texas,

Cold water slows bass activity, so your fishing will need to be slower and more deliberate. Crankbaits, jigs, and spoons are the best lure choices, depending on the cover and the structure you're fishing.

guide, once caught a 17-pound bass from Lake Fork and kept it alive in an aquarium; the bass did not eat anything during its first full month of captivity and remained healthy, so we know bass can do without food for long periods of time.

This is also why bass tend to stay in large schools during the winter months. Their primary consideration is not food but comfort. The bass gather where the temperature is most agreeable to them. Sometimes the most comfortable water is extremely deep, too. Randy Fite, one of the best deep water anglers I know, has caught fish deeper than 70 feet.

What's amazing is that a rise in water temperature of just three or four degrees is often all that's needed to make bass become active again. Thus, winter fishing on sunny days is usually better in the afternoon hours; the water temperature has risen just enough to rejuvenate the fish.

You'd think, then, that in warm water the fish's metabolism would simply continue to run faster and faster the higher the temperature rose, but such is not the case. In fact, it starts slowing dramatically at about 80 degrees. The reason is because warmer water contains less oxygen, so the higher the temperature the more difficulty the bass has surviving.

This is one reason vegetation is not always the most productive place to fish in the heat of summer. On some lakes, grass beds can produce awesome midday summer stringers, but if you check the records, you'll nearly always see the vegetation is in deeper water, which in itself contains more oxygen.

To use Lake Fork in Texas as another example, the best fishing in spring and early summer takes place along the grasslines in the tributary creeks in eight to 12 feet of water. By mid to late June, however, you have to move to the main lake grasslines in 12 to 15 feet if you want to catch any fish. Water temperature and oxygen content are the reasons.

Bass certainly leave their preferred comfort zones to feed. You have undoubtedly noticed that shallow water fishing is often good early and late each day in the summer but that sloping channel banks are often more productive the rest of the day. The bass move in and then move out again.

This is also why night fishing is most productive during the summer months—water temperatures may not be optimum in the shallows after dark but they're certainly more agreeable than during the daylight hours. And, as every night fisherman knows, fishing action is rarely steady during a night; it happens in flurries as bass are moving up from deeper water to feed.

FISH SLOWLY IN COLD WATER

The basic fishing rules with regard to water temperature are simple but they certainly are not set in stone. In cold water, because the bass are sluggish and will not chase lures very actively, it's important to choose lures you can fish very slowly and leave in the strike zone. I enjoy using a jig with a big pork trailer hopped very deliberately around bottom cover, but this isn't all you can use.

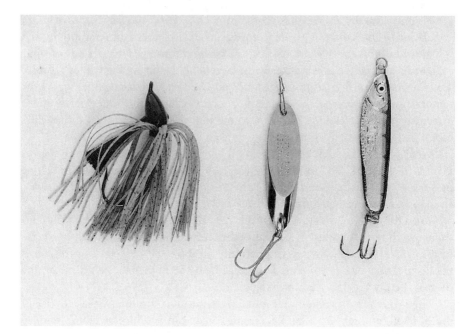

Jigging spoons (middle and right) can be made to imitate injured or dying shad when worked with proper rod action, and they are extremely effective cold weather lures. Regular jigs (left), many times rigged with a pork chunk attached, are also good, productive cold water lures.

Spinnerbaits can also be effective but they're hard to use because you have to fish them both deep and slowly. That means using a heavier head with smaller blades so the lure doesn't have as much lift.

Still another cold-water lure choice is a crankbait. If you're fishing around heavy cover such as fallen trees and stumps, this is a lure that can bring surprising results. Choose a lure with a wide, pronounced wobbling action and which dives to mid-depth ranges (10 to 15 feet). You want one that will run this deep because it will be easier to keep down near the bottom with a slower retrieve.

JIGGING SPOON A POPULAR COLD-WATER LURE

Perhaps the most popular of all cold-water, deep-water lures is the jigging spoon. Once bass are located with a depthfinder, a ½- or ¾-ounce spoon can be fished vertically over the side of the boat and lowered to the precise depth of the fish. The lure is then jumped or hopped up and down with rod tip action; different action should be tried until the fish are triggered into biting.

When you're using cold-water jigging spoons, remember that a little rod tip action can make a spoon jump upward a long way, and bass may not want that much movement. Just two or three inches of rod movement are sometimes all that's needed to catch them.

Remember, also, that a jigging spoon looks more natural when it falls on a slack line, so once you complete your upward jigging motion, lower your rod tip quickly to allow the spoon to drop and swing from side to side. Most strikes come as the spoon is falling, so learn to watch your line where it enters the water for any type of movement that might signal a hit.

FIND WARMEST WATER

When the water temperature is really cold, I look for the warmest water I can find. This will generally be clearer water (sunlight penetration warms clear water faster than dingy water), which usually means anywhere from midlake to the lower end.

Make sure you check the temperature in different creeks, because invariably you'll find one several degrees warmer than the rest. Look at riprap or rocky bluffs that absorb and hold heat and help attract bass, and if you have an especially accurate lake map it may even have the location of a spring pinpointed.

Sometimes vegetation will hold bass reasonably shallow in cold water. In fact, I have seen times when a topwater chugger fished over mossbeds brought bass up for vicious strikes in frigid temperatures.

Jigs worked slowly along the outside edges or in the potholes are also worth trying, and if the vegetation is several feet below the surface but fairly thick on the bottom (shown by your depthfinder) then slow rolling a spinnerbait over the top of the greenery is another option.

As I said earlier, sudden temperature changes affect bass the hardest, and these are most noticeable in the fall and winter. In fact, the first hard, freezing cold front of autumn is always one of the worst because it stops the warming cycle of summer and starts the cooling cycle of winter. Bass will leave shallow water quickly for deeper depths until they become adjusted to the change.

The Sam Rayburn tournament experience isn't the only time I've had to deal with bass that moved because of a sudden cold front, and if you fish long enough, you'll experience the same things I have. That's why when I know the possibility of a cold front exists during a tournament, I look for the places bass are most likely to move to after it hits. Nearby ditches and channels are some of the best places to look, because water temperatures remain more stable in deeper depths. Don't be surprised if the bass move 100 yards or more to reach such a sanctuary, because they'll do it. Thick vegetation is another key spot to look, especially in spring if a front hits after the bass have left the vegetation for the clearer shallows to spawn. If it gets really cold, a lot of the fish will move back to the edge of the grass.

Because waters warm slowly, they do not change bass behavior rapidly. This is not to say bass activity can't change overnight, because sometimes it does. I still wonder what happened to a school of fish I found on Lake Okeechobee during practice for a tournament several years ago.

Contrary to all the rules about shallow water bass in hot weather, I had located some enormous fish in shallow water near the West Wall. How big? Well, my first cast brought in a 9-pounder, and 50 feet later I caught an 8-pounder. In one 300-yard stretch I caught seven bass between 6 and 9 pounds. Of course, I was ecstatic. These were the kind of bass you lie awake at night dreaming about, and I certainly dreamed about them that night, and I have dreamed about them ever since. My first bass of the morning weighed over 8½ pounds, but it was the last big fish I ever caught there. Instead, I caught dozens of smaller bass under 2 pounds. In three hard days of fishing that area and the water surrounding it, I never did locate those monster bass again.

What happened? I don't know for certain, but I feel fairly sure temperature and oxygen levels had something to do with it. Oxygen levels can change quickly because of photosynthesis, or the lack of it, and when it does change, big bass are always the first to stop biting.

IN SUMMER FIND COLDEST WATER

In hot weather, you simply reverse the procedure you follow in winter. You look for cooler water, and this can come in several locations.

Vegetation is a place to look, but not necessarily shallow vegetation. Remember what I said earlier about Lake Fork. If vegetation completely blocks sunlight penetration to the water below, underwater vegetation and algae will die and use up the available oxygen. In its place they produce carbon dioxide, which will force bass to relocate.

In warm weather, shallow water fishing is normally best early and late when temperatures are more comfortable and light is less intense. Bass will stay tighter to any available cover the rest of the day.

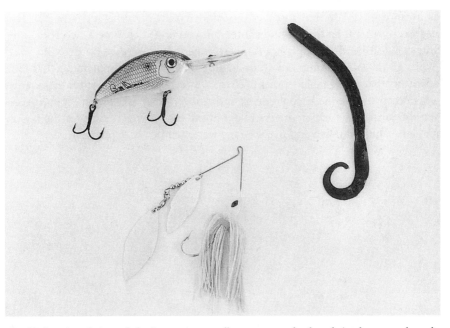

Crankbaits, spinnerbaits, and plastic worms are excellent warm-weather lure choices because each can be fished with a variety of retrieves to suit the moods of the bass. Because these lures are also sensitive to motion, they are good lures to use if you're fishing in current.

So, if you're going to fish summer vegetation, fish it early in the morning or later in the afternoon when bass have moved in to feed. Concentrate in deeper vegetation during the heat of the day. In the deeper grass, a favorite fishing technique I often use is to drop a heavy ¾- or 1-ounce jig through the vegetation into the relatively open water underneath. I jump the lure pretty aggressively several times to attract the bass, then reel in for another pitch to a new spot if I don't get a strike.

Another good place to look for warm water bass is in the upper end of a lake where it usually turns into a river and current is present. Moving water is cooler and has more oxygen than stable, calm water, so the bass there will be more active. I like to fish crankbaits down behind rocks and stumps, retrieving them with the current, or perhaps drifting plastic worms or jigs into the same places.

On the upper reaches of Lake Norman where the Catawba River still has current, I often fish a spinnerbait because there is plenty of cover along the channel banks. Again, however, the best retrieve is one where I bring my lure downstream with the current and bumping the cover.

WINDY SHORELINES GOOD IN THE FALL

In the fall, windy shorelines can be great places to fish, but they're not nearly as good during the summer. That's because wind can warm a shoreline just as easily as it can cool it. You may discover the windy bank you're fishing is four or five degrees warmer than the upwind shore, so if you don't get some action soon after you start fishing, don't stay on a windy summer bank.

In all of your fishing and study of water temperature, remember that bass adapt to what is available to them. There are certainly places within their range where the water remains cool year-round, and in other areas where it stays constantly warm. Use the parameters I have given as a basic guideline for the region and lake where you fish and measure the water temperature often.

6

BASS AND THE WEATHER

No matter where or when you go bass fishing, you're going to be influenced by the weather. You may have to wear a rainsuit for rain or a snowmobile suit for cold. A gusting wind may make boat control nearly impossible, while a bright, hot sky may make you think more about swimming than fishing.

Not surprisingly, bass are also influenced by weather factors. The ways they are influenced are not always predictable, and often not understood, either. Changing weather may also trigger a chain of events, so what is actually influencing the bass—the precipitation, the wind, or the phase of the moon?

As a bass fisherman, your best preparation for these weather changes is experience—time on the water. Each experience you have provides another reference to draw on in the future, and experience may well help other bass fishermen in a future generation, because we certainly don't know all the answers now.

BAROMETRIC PRESSURE

The influence of barometric pressure is quite possibly the least understood factor in all of bass fishing, and it is also probably the most baffling because as humans we seldom physically feel barometric pressure changes. Many theories have been given as to why bass act a particular way when the barometer has reached a certain level, but no one has ever given a satisfactory answer as to why.

A lot of fishermen don't really know what barometric pressure is. The proper term is atmospheric pressure and it is simply a measurement of the weight of air, with dry air being heavier than wet air. The air is measured in a barometer, a glass tube slightly more than 30 inches long and partially filled with mercury.

At sea level, the average height of the mercury in the tube is between 29 and 30 inches; thus, virtually every barometric pressure reading you ever hear will be within this range. Heavier, drier air pushes the mercury higher; lighter, wetter air makes the mercury stay lower. Now you can understand why a high barometer basically indicates dry, stable conditions while a low barometer indicates wet weather.

Essentially, the rule of thumb about barometric pressure and fishing is that bass bite best when the barometer falls fast or rises fast. Fishing is also good when the barometer is stable and steady, wherever it is. Fishing is toughest on a slow fall, or when the barometer is extremely high or extremely low.

Fishermen learn by watching the barometer, because its movement influences bass behavior. A falling or rising barometer are among the best times to fish, although action often slows when the barometer is high.

My personal feeling about the barometer is to be aware of it and what it does to the bass and means to the weather in general. Barometric changes basically signal an impending weather change; an approaching storm makes the barometer fall while a departing storm lets it rise again.

Initially, fishing can be very good when the barometer first begins dropping. Then it will become increasingly more difficult. After the front or the storm, the skies clear and the barometer begins rising and fishing steadily improves. You have no control over the barometer, however, so do not let it rule your fishing entirely.

One of the changes a falling barometer often brings is rain, and bass fishermen rarely complain about having to fish in a slow, light drizzle. Light rain means gray skies and a dimpled water surface, which seems to make bass more active.

One theory is that the fish are not as spooky and tend to be roaming more; I think this is true, but that it applies to baitfish as well. Whenever they're active, bass are also active.

Some of my biggest stringers have been caught during a light drizzle, and most have come with a spinnerbait. Crankbaits are also excellent choices but topwater lures like buzz baits or chuggers are not nearly as effective, possibly because they can't be seen as well on the surface.

HEAVY RAIN

Heavy rains with thunder and lightning are a different story. Fishing is rarely good during a drenching downpour, but is it because of the rain or the lightning? My own thoughts are lightning probably disrupts the fish more than the rain. I do know prolonged periods of unsettled weather that include thunderstorms, boiling clouds, a little sunshine, then another round or two of storms, nearly always produce poor fishing.

If the rains are long enough and heavy enough to cause a lake to rise, then bass nearly always tend to rise with the water, moving into newly flooded areas along the shoreline. This is one place where food is usually most abundant, since the running water will wash insects and other food into the lake.

Rising water also scatters bass. When I'm faced with these types of conditions, I tie on a spinnerbait and start working the shoreline pretty fast, making my casts right to the edge of the water and retrieving the lure just a few inches below the surface.

I fished a tournament on Truman Lake in Missouri several years ago in which the water came up so fast it was nearly impossible to keep up with it; the "new" shoreline kept moving back and cover continually disappeared as the water rose! I've been in other tournaments where the water rose two to three feet overnight, and, needless to say, scattered the fish in all directions as they enjoyed a bonanza of new food.

MUDDY WATER

Muddy water can be another by-product of heavy rain, and it will also cause bass to relocate. Initially, the water will become "stained," and if it stays this way, you can still catch bass by working a big spinnerbait or crankbait through it. Visibility is reduced so use lures that make a lot of vibrations.

When the water becomes truly muddy, it's time to look for clear water. At times you can catch bass right along the mud line, the dividing line between the muddy water and the clear. If it is a distinct line, you may have some success with a crankbait right along the very edge of it.

When you're forced to look for clear water, don't overlook the very backs of creeks. Tributaries are the first to muddy, and they're among the first places to clear, too. You may also find small pockets or coves of clear water along a main lake shoreline, especially in the lower end. For awhile you can actually get ahead of the muddy water.

Still another possibility for clear water is in the far upper end of the lake, possibly just below a dam. In unstable conditions, the best fishing often occurs in moving water or current.

In all of these clear water spots, water temperature and available cover and depth will usually determine your lure choice. Spinnerbaits, crankbaits, Carolina rigs, and jigs are all lures to consider.

WIND

Sooner or later in your fishing career you'll encounter wind, either during a heavy rain or perhaps under a clear sky. A light breeze, like a drizzle, often improves fishing dramatically. Bass may become active almost immediately, leaving cover and moving into shallow water.

I think one of the reasons bass do become more active is because a rippled water surface forms a type of protection, since the bass can't be seen nearly as well from above. Bass do not have many predators, but those they do have often strike from above.

Again, lure choices usually depend on water temperature and cover. This could be a good time to try a topwater lure, especially something with propellers. Crankbaits and spinnerbaits also work well. Remember, when fish are active, try to catch them first with an "active" lure. If you don't get any results, change to a Carolina rig or possibly a jig.

When the wind is really howling and the lake is churned into waves, boat control and casting become two of your biggest problems. Fishing action, however, can at times be spectacular.

What happens, particularly after wind has been constant for a day or two, is that baitfish are repositioned and the bass follow them. Fishermen often say the wind blows baitfish up on points or against bluffs, but this isn't really what happens.

A slight breeze that ripples the water often improves fishing, but when the wind makes open water fishing too difficult, consider moving to shallow cover and flipping and pitching.

Waves caused by wind will wash some baitfish out of cover but primarily, wind blows plankton, not only from the surface but also from below the surface, in a process known as upwelling. Eventually the plankton concentrates along some obstacle, usually a windy shoreline, bluff, or point, and the baitfish soon follow. Then the bass arrive to feed on the baitfish.

In a word, your lure choice here should be a crankbait. You may have to position your boat so you're casting into the wind and retrieving with the waves, but it can be worth it. I've experienced windblown bluffs where every cast brought a fish.

SNOW

Surprisingly, bass fishing can be good during snowstorms. During an April 1983 tournament on the Chickahominy River in Virginia, a sudden snowstorm caught us by surprise, but the bass kept right on biting—on buzzbaits! Several years later, during a tournament on Lake Martin in Alabama where we encountered snow and sleet, the bass wanted a fast-moving spinnerbait.

What's happening to cause this? I don't believe anyone has the real answer, but it's probably several different things. First, the sky is normally overcast during a snowfall, so the fish are more active, and secondly, perhaps they go on a feeding binge in preparation for colder, more severe weather ahead. Many animals do this.

MOON PHASES

Although they aren't a weather factor, I want to discuss moon phases here because the moon definitely affects bass behavior. Generally speaking, the moon's first quarter produces average fishing, and the half moon to the full moon produces better action. Most anglers who have kept diaries of their fishing have noticed these same results.

Some of your best fishing will also occur whenever you have a full or nearly full moon visible in the sky at the same time the sun is up. Normally, the early morning hours before 9 a.m. are the prime time. We noticed most of the big bass—those between 8 and 10 pounds—caught during the 1995 Texas Bassmaster Invitational on Sam Rayburn were caught in the morning when the full moon was still up.

Many years ago, a fisherman named John Alden Knight produced what he called the first Solunar Tables, in which he theorized that bass feed more actively during certain periods of tidal activity, which we know the moon controls. Knight's tables have two "major" and two "minor" feeding periods lasting more than an hour during each 24-hour period.

These tables, and others developed since, are essentially tide charts adjusted to various time zones and longitudes across the United States. It's easy to explain what they are but no one can explain why there is some validity to them.

I take notes of when the major periods occur but I do not really adjust my fishing for them. I'm on the water eight to 10 hours a day so I'm fishing through the majors, minors, and in between. Sometimes, if it is convenient, I'll try to be in one of my best areas when a major feeding period occurs, but not always.

The problem with depending too heavily on the Solunar Tables is that many other factors can also influence bass behavior, as we've discussed. Rain, wind, barometric pressure, heat, water temperature, cloud cover, and baitfish activity all contribute to how a bass acts.

Jack Wingate caught this Lake Seminole bass by letting his spinnerbait hit the tree stump as he made the retrieve. I change every retrieve I make with a spinnerbait until I learn how bass want the lure presented.

7

LURE PRESENTATION

Of all the factors that can separate amateur anglers from experienced bass pros, probably the most obvious is lure presentation. Cast after cast, hour after hour, the most successful tournament anglers will put their lures right beside stumps and logs, underneath overhanging brush, or precisely along a channel break. I don't mean generally close to these targets. I mean putting a spinnerbait into a coffee cup-sized opening in a brush pile 20 feet away, or dropping a jig into a saucer-sized opening in a grass bed—while you're controlling the boat in wind.

This is what it takes to be competitive in the sport today, because these are the types of places bass are hiding. Bass are basically cover- or object-oriented, and as you'll soon discover, they do not often move very far from that cover to chase and strike a lure.

Thus, one of my primary rules of lure presentation is to make sure I'm always casting at something. This can be as big as a log or as small as a single twig.

The distance a bass will move to hit a lure is called the strike zone, and it changes depending on the mood of the fish. Generally, however, you should always assume it is a very small area around the piece of cover the fish is using. That's why accurate lure presentation is so important. You can be in an area containing a lot of bass, but if you don't get your lures right in front of them you may never get a strike.

I also believe bass are a lot spookier than most anglers think, and a bad lure presentation simply puts the fish on alert. A lure that crashes down right beside a stump where a bass may be hiding will often send that fish fleeing as fast as possible.

The area around the cover you're fishing is known as potentially productive water, but the term also includes other pieces of cover nearby. Basically, it's where additional bass might be. Along a shoreline, productive water may extend out four or five feet from the bass. If you've maneuvered your boat into the middle of a stump field, productive water could be anywhere you cast and retrieve your lure.

KEEP THE LURE IN PRODUCTIVE WATER

Thus, in addition to getting your lure close to a specific target to enter a strike zone, you should strive to keep that lure in productive water during as much of the retrieve as possible.

Flipping and pitching are two important lure presentations every serious bass angler needs to learn. Both techniques allow quiet and precise lure delivery into heavy cover normal casting seldom reaches.

You can do this several ways, depending on the type of cover you're fishing. Along a grassline, for example, bass frequently hold along an outside edge. To keep your lure in this productive water the maximum amount of time during your retrieve, you should consider casting parallel to that edge rather than straight toward it at a perpendicular angle.

How close to that edge should your parallel cast be? As close as you can get it, at least until you locate the fish. This is what casting accuracy and lure presentation are all about. A cast four feet away from that edge may never catch a fish.

When you're fishing individual targets such as stumps, potentially productive water actually extends beyond the stump. Just imagine the stump sitting in the center of a circle that might have a radius of as much as four feet. This is another reason your lure should not land precisely at the stump, but rather, three to four feet beyond it.

This keeps your lure in potentially productive water for possibly as much as eight feet as you retrieve to the stump and past it, but you accomplish something else at the same time: assuming the bass is holding tight beside that stump, your lure doesn't frighten the fish by landing on top of him. Instead, your lure swims into the strike zone, which appears much more natural.

Even this type of careful casting, however, won't always be enough to generate a strike. I firmly believe, and so do a lot of other top pros I know, bass can become accustomed to seeing or hearing certain lures and stop striking them. This is purely an effect of fishing pressure, and I'm not surprised it happens.

I see it often in tournaments. An angler leads the first two days but fades the third day and loses the tournament. The common complaint is "My fish deserted me," but I don't think that's what really happened. I believe the angler's fish simply turned off to the lure he was using because they saw it so much.

Rick Clunn, winner of four Bass Masters Classics, related an interesting story to me that happened during his third Classic win, the 1984 championship on the Arkansas River. Clunn won with a record catch of 75 pounds, 9 ounces, but few people know that on the third morning, after he already caught more than 45 pounds of fish from one spot, the bass absolutely refused to hit his crankbait.

Instead of changing techniques, Clunn simply changed to a different type of crankbait, one with a very tight wobbling vibration, in contrast to the wide wobbling lure he'd been using. The bass liked it, and by afternoon's end the Texas pro had caught more than 27 pounds, the heaviest stringer of the week!

Changing lures as Clunn did is one way to try to overcome the reluctance of bass to hit a familiar lure. This particular phase of lure presentation is gaining a lot of converts in the pro ranks; one of the favorite techniques is using deep-diving crankbaits instead of spinnerbaits in shallow water, just because the bass haven't seen as many of them.

CHANGING RETRIEVES

Another type of lure presentation that should always be tried is simply changing retrieves. You speed up your retrieve, you slow it down, you stop and go. What this creates is something abnormal or different, and often it generates a strike.

I don't have a "normal" retrieve with a spinnerbait, for example, nor should you. Don't ever just cast and wind a spinnerbait right back to you. One of the things I do on every spinnerbait cast is to pull the lure toward me with the rod as soon as it hits the water. To me, this makes the lure sound like something alive that just fell in and is trying to escape.

I believe 80 percent of the strikes we get from bass are purely reaction strikes. The fish is not looking and deciding whether or not to strike; it simply does out of instinct. Get in the habit of varying your retrieve every cast; soon it will become natural for you, and you'll notice you're also catching more fish.

BOUNCE OFF A STUMP

Another technique we use is to hit the cover with our lures. Remember that stump with the imaginary four foot circle of productive water around it? As you retrieve your lure, let it bounce into the stump, or glance off one side. Again, you're creating an unnatural occurrence.

One of the unnatural impressions you can create is that of an injured baitfish. You can let your spinnerbaits "die" or fall right into the stump, and you can let your crankbaits hesitate for a moment after they hit a stick or limb. I can't tell you how many tournaments have been won by anglers who used these techniques.

If you believe a particular target holds bass, don't leave after just two or three casts that don't draw strikes. Sometimes it takes a dozen or more to make a fish hit. I once watched from my boat as a friend made 15 casts to the same log with a crankbait before he caught a bass.

CHANGE THE ANGLE

Changing the angle of your retrieve frequently brings a strike. I remember working down a great looking brushy shoreline once in a tournament but not getting a single strike. It was just too good a place to leave, so I turned the boat around and went right back through the same water from the opposite direction. I never changed spinnerbaits, but you'd have thought I had just discovered virgin water. For some reason, the bass along that bank preferred a lure coming at that particular angle rather than from my original direction.

This is why the technique of "fan-casting" is so important, especially when you're fishing points. When we begin fishing, we don't know exactly where the fish are or how they're positioned. That's what we try to determine, and fan-casting does this. With your boat facing the point, you can aim casts from the ten o'clock position all the way to two o'clock, then move a short distance and repeat the sequence.

Sometimes repeated casts to the same target may be needed to generate a strike. Use different retrieves and cast from different angles if you really believe a bass is present.

You can even do this to some extent on individual targets. Let's go back to that single stump still another time. You can cast on the left side, then the right side. After you move forward a few feet in the boat, the angle of your presentation will change completely and you can make several more casts on either side.

Sometimes, however, repeated casting like this still won't bring a strike. Perhaps the strike zone is so small and the fish so unaggressive the only way you can catch them is by putting a lure right in front of them and leaving it there.

Two ways you can do this are with the techniques of flipping and pitching, and among tournament bass anglers, these are two of the most important lure presentations that can be learned. Flipping drops a lure, usually a worm or jig, into thick cover just a few feet from the boat. Pitching is basically long-range flipping into heavy cover with the same lures.

RODS AND LINES FOR FLIPPING

Flipping requires a long rod, generally a 7½ footer, with a fairly stiff or heavy action because you encounter bass at close quarters and also have to bring them out of the cover. Lines used for flipping range from 25-pound-test up to 40-pound-test, and some use braided lines that are even stronger. The advantages of flipping are that the technique presents a lure into thick cover that ordinary casts probably could not reach, and it presents the lure very quietly so a fish is not frightened.

Here's how you do it. With your rod in your right hand and reel in freespool, pull about seven feet of line out so your lure dangles right by the reel when the rod

Pitching and flipping are two lure presentations often used when bass have a small strike zone and are holding tight to cover. Both provide extreme accuracy and a quiet lure entry into the water.

is held vertically. Now, pull another arm's length of line off the reel with your left hand and hold it to the side. Pick a target within four or five feet and lower your rod so it points at the target, then quickly raise it again in a gentle arc. This pendulum movement will cause the lure to swing out to the target. As it does, feed the line in your left hand to the rod so the lure carries it out too. As the lure swings to the target, gradually lower your rod again so you lessen the distance the lure falls into the water. This is how the quiet entry presentation is accomplished. As the lure begins to sink, you can pull line off the reel so the lure falls vertically. Click the reel back into gear (many reels have flipping levers that do this automatically), then jig your lure up and down a time or two in the cover. If you don't get a strike, retrieve the lure by raising the rod tip and pulling line out with your left hand again.

Describing flipping like this makes it seem much more difficult than it really is. All you need to become an excellent flipper is practice, and you can do it in your living room. More than a few pros I know put a bowl or paper cup out in front of them and practice during the winter months when they're not out on the water. Another way to learn, of course, is to have a friend demonstrate and show you.

PITCHING

If you can flip, then you can pitch. You may want to change rods so you have a more flexible tip because the tip is what really helps send the lure out 20 or 30 feet and beyond. The primary difference is that instead of holding extra line in your left hand, you start by holding the lure.

Lower the rod with the tip pointing at the target, then swing it upward with a firm but smooth underhand motion. Let the lure go as you do, and control the freespooling line with your thumb as on a regular cast. Again, with practice you'll be able to put lures—any lure, not just jigs and worms—into tiny openings you might never reach with a cast.

One key to successful pitching is keeping your lure close to the water as it moves toward the target. If your lure arcs high, you're holding the lure too long before releasing it, and you're probably raising your rod tip too high. Distance is not accomplished by how high you raise your rod, but rather, how fast you raise it. You also need the spool tension on your reel to be as loose as possible.

Pitching is really good when you're in clear water and the bass are spooky so you have to stay farther away from them, as well as when you want to get lures underneath overhanging branches. Good pitchers can drop their lures into tiny openings with hardly a ripple.

SKIPPING

Sometimes neither flipping or pitching will get your lure where it needs to be. I'm speaking here primarily of reaching those dark, shadowy places far underneath boathouses. The lure presentation that accomplishes this is known as skipping, in which you cast so your lure bounces or skips several times on the surface as it travels under the boathouse.

Most anglers learn skipping first with a spinning reel because it's easier. Plastic worms are the most often used lure, too, with the sinker pegged right above the hook. What's needed is a sharp, sidearm type cast so the lure's trajectory is flat, low to the water, and fast.

For best results, the lure should hit the water the first time near the edge of the target. That way, you'll get maximum distance underneath the boathouse with the following skips. I suggest you learn the basics of rod and reel control by first practicing out in open water. It isn't a difficult technique, but it takes more practice than flipping or pitching.

I'm sure bass hit lures for a variety of reasons, but it's hard to determine just what those reasons are. In human terms we often say bass strike because of hunger, in anger, out of reflex, and perhaps in territorial defense. The actual reason bass strike isn't really important. What is important is realizing that something in your lure presentation triggered a response.

Pay attention to each cast and retrieve you make, because when you do get a strike, you want to be able to recognize what you were doing that caused that response. Believe it or not, your lure presentation is frequently a major part of a bass catching pattern.

8

Spinnerbaits Shallow and Deep

Of all the lures we use to catch bass, the spinnerbait ranks as one of the most unusual. That's because it doesn't look like anything a bass sees or eats naturally. At the same time it is a lure that catches bass year-round; it's a lure that can be fished shallow or deep, fast or slow; and it's a lure that catches big bass. Of the 41 largemouths over 10 pounds I have caught in my life, 29 have come on a spinnerbait.

Although spinnerbaits have been around in various designs since the 1920s, the true "safety pin" configuration we use most often today—a molded leadhead and hook on one wire shaft and one or two spinner blades on an opposing wire shaft—first became available in the early 1950s. While this basic design is standard, dozens of variations are available and even more choices are produced each year.

For example, spinnerbaits are made in weight ranging from about ¼ to a over 2 ounces; blade designs include not only the time-honored Colorado and willowleaf, but several other manufacturers' designs, and now they're colored too. Skirts also come in a wide range of colors and materials that weren't even dreamed of just a few years ago.

I've been fishing spinnerbaits since the early 1960s when I was guiding at Santee-Cooper. That's where Roland Martin and I became good friends, and one day he showed me the first spinnerbait I ever saw. It looked like a small black bug with a spinner; it was a little ⅜-ounce lure with a size 4 Colorado blade. Roland wouldn't let me use it because it was the only one he had, but a month later he had made some himself and sent me a white one. The first day I took it out on Lake Moultrie around Leroy's Landing I caught 10 bass over 5 pounds, including one about 9. I lost a lot of fish because it had just a little 1/0 hook, but I was more concerned about losing the lure than losing fish, since it was the only one I had.

That day was all it took for me to become a spinnerbait fisherman. In the 30 years since, I have tried to learn as much as I could about this amazing lure, and I'm still learning.

YOU MUST FEEL THE VIBRATIONS

I believe the most critical aspect of spinnerbait fishing is being able to feel the blades vibrating. This is how you stay in contact with the lure, how you know it's

One of the earliest of the "safety pin" spinnerbaits was the Houser "Hell Diver," which appeared on the market in the early 1950s. Other spinnerbaits utilizing different designs appeared as early as the 1920s.

working for you. When you don't feel the blades vibrating, you should be able to set the hook because it means a bass has it. Unfortunately, many fishermen don't realize the importance of feeling those blades, and I see them casting and winding hour after hour but only catching a small percentage of the bass they might otherwise get. If you want to become a serious bass fisherman, you absolutely have to develop and recognize this sense of feel.

Not being able to feel blades vibrate is usually caused by two things—either the lure is poorly designed and the blades are not turning, or your rod action is much too heavy and your sensitivity is lost.

CHOOSING A SPINNERBAIT

When you're looking at spinnerbaits, make certain you get one in which the lower blade is attached by a ball bearing swivel. This is what lets the blade spin with the slightest motion. If you hold the lure and blow on it gently, the blade will spin freely; a non-ball bearing swivel will turn a few times, then stop.

As for rod actions, I use either a 6- or 6½-foot medium or medium-heavy rod, depending on the weight of the spinnerbaits. These rods have very sensitive tips that actually vibrate as I retrieve the spinnerbait, so even if I don't feel a strike I know something has happened when I see the tip stop vibrating.

Today, choosing a spinnerbait is a lot harder than it was years ago, simply because there are so many more models on the market. When you're studying which spinnerbait to use, it's important to understand the relationship between the head weight and the blade size, because this is what really determines how the lure can be used.

COLORADO BLADES GOOD FOR COOL WATER

First, remember that the rounded teardrop-shaped Colorado blades produce better vibration than the more elongated willowleaf blades. Colorado blades are made in sizes ranging from a small size 1 up to about a big size 8. The most popular are sizes 3 and 4. I like to use Colorado blades in cooler water because they're easy to fish slow and still feel their vibration. I also like to use them in dingy or murky water, and at night. Normally I fish two Colorado blades rather than one unless bass are extremely spooky, when I'll just use a single small blade.

WILLOWLEAF BLADES GOOD FOR VEGETATION

Willowleaf blades do not have the strong vibrations Colorado blades have but they produce more flash and they're better blades for vegetation because they don't get clogged as easily. They are made in sizes 1 to about 7, but I rarely ever use one larger than size 6 because they're difficult to cast with any accuracy. The big blades catch wind and nearly stop the lure in midair.

One of my favorite spinnerbaits uses a size 3 Colorado blade ahead of a size 4½ willowleaf. A lot of tournament fishermen like this combination because it produces both flash and vibration, works well in cover, and casts easily.

In the late 1970s I was testing some lures with Jim Bagley in a tank he had wired with audio equipment. With ear phones we could listen to the vibrations various lures made as well as watch that vibration pattern on a special monitor. We were comparing those vibrations to the vibrations produced by shad that were also swimming in the tank. My spinnerbait with the Colorado and willowleaf blades very closely matched the shad vibrations, so it's been one of my favorite lures ever since. I use this combination on spinnerbaits from ⅜ to ¾ ounce.

Although most spinnerbait blades are furnished to lure manufacturers by one company, some spinnerbait makers are beginning to produce their own blade designs as they search for more vibration, more flash, or both. Personally, I think there is a lot of room for development in this particular area, and I think this is where most new spinnerbait development will occur in the future.

At certain times of the year, particularly in the spring and again in the fall, it may be important to match blade size with the size of the bait bass are feeding on. It's also important to match blade size with the aggressiveness of the bass; the less active the bass are, the smaller the blades you should use.

SPINNERBAIT BLADES CREATE LIFT

Here, however, is where trouble often enters the picture. All spinnerbait blades, Colorado or willowleaf, create lift and cause a spinnerbait to rise. The larger the blade, the more lift it will create, and the faster you retrieve the lure, the quicker and higher it will rise.

If you want big blades for flash or vibration in deep water, you have to retrieve the spinnerbait very slowly, but at times, such as in clear, warm water, bass may be deep but still want a fast-moving lure. This is when you have to change to a heavier lure and smaller blades.

A good choice for fishing deep and slow is a ¾-ounce spinnerbait with a big size 6 Colorado blade or perhaps a size 6 willowleaf with a slightly smaller Colorado blade ahead of it. I use a ¾-ounce spinnerbait when fishing submerged grass beds down to about eight feet or so, and then change to a 1-ounce model if I'm fishing down to about 15 feet.

This technique of fishing spinnerbaits slow is known as "slow rolling" and it's one of my favorites. I don't limit it to deep water either. In early spring when the water is cold and the bass aren't really aggressive, I may slow roll a spinnerbait in four feet of water. Slow rolling is simply a very slow retrieve in which the spinnerbait is kept in contact with cover on or near the bottom. You simply crawl the lure over limbs, just barely touch the top of grass, or let the lure slip over the edge of a channel drop.

In shallow water, you don't want to use a heavy lure if you have to make a slow retrieve. At the same time, using larger blades will help keep the lure up if you have to retrieve fast. Sometimes when I want to cover a lot of water in a hurry, especially if I'm fishing over submerged vegetation, I'll use a ¾-ounce spinnerbait with a size 2 Colorado blade ahead of a size 6 willowleaf. The reason a heavier spinnerbait usually works better under such conditions is that big blades can overpower a light lure. Instead of coming straight and smooth through the water, big blades will cause the lure to roll over and when it does, bass won't hit it.

At the same time, bass may want a small but fast-moving spinnerbait in shallow or deep water, to match the size of the bait they're feeding on. You may find yourself using a ¼-ounce lure more than you ever suspected, so don't underestimate the fish attraction these smaller spinnerbaits have.

Very often, switching to a smaller spinnerbait size will catch bass when other larger spinnerbaits won't. Part of this may be the fickleness of bass in general, but more and more I think bass become accustomed to seeing and hearing spinnerbaits and begin to shy away from them at certain times. A smaller lure not only produces a different vibration, but also may not seem quite as threatening to them.

VARY YOUR RETRIEVES

Another aspect of spinnerbait fishing I feel is often overlooked is the simple act of retrieving. Each retrieve you make should be different until you determine what triggers a bass into striking. For the most part, spinnerbaits draw instinct strikes, so don't continue to make the same retrieve over and over.

If the water is fairly warm—my favorite temperature range is between 55 and 65 degrees—I'll often start with a fast retrieve that keeps the lure six to eight inches below the surface. If I don't get any strikes, I'll gradually slow the lure and fish it deeper. Then, I'll gently touch the cover I'm fishing with my retrieve. I do not crash the lure into a brush pile but just bump it gently.

Once, when I was filming a spinnerbait fishing video, I made five or six casts around a brush pile, never touching any of the limbs, and I never had a strike. On the next cast, I let the spinnerbait hit a limb and a 6-pounder exploded out to hit the lure. I'm convinced that fish hit purely out of instinct because it felt some type of injured prey had just bumped into the limb.

Sometimes bass want the lure retrieved fast. This often occurs in clear water, and I've seen it in both summer and winter. Normally, a fast retrieve is preferable because it doesn't give bass a chance to really see the lure; it takes advantage of the instinct strikes.

"Buzzing" spinnerbaits like this in clear water where the lure stays just below the surface usually produces best when done close to cover or structure, such as rock bluffs, over fast falling points, or even along bridge abutments and riprap. This is where bass suspend, and the churning lure brings them up.

Spinnerbaits work well in heavy, shallow cover because they're basically weedless and can be retrieved quickly. Here Hank Parker uses a spinnerbait in the thick timber of Missouri's Truman Lake.

DEPTH IS A KEY FACTOR WITH SPINNERBAITS

Of those 29 bass over 10 pounds that I've caught on a spinnerbait, all but two came from water less than six feet deep. I think depth is another key to successful spinnerbait fishing. This is primarily a shallow-water lure, and it's a target lure. You need to be throwing at something specific every cast when you're working shallow. In my experience, the first 10 feet of water out from the shoreline are the most productive.

This is not to say you can't fish a spinnerbait deep, as in the case of slow rolling. I've caught bass as deep as 25 feet on a spinnerbait, but I believe the lure's efficiency—or ours—falls off rapidly when we fish deeper than about 15 feet. Once you move into those depths, Carolina rigs, and possibly crankbaits, become more efficient lures to use.

One technique I've seen work numerous times in tournament competition is to slow roll spinnerbaits down steep banks. This is a good cold-water technique when conditions are unstable, but again, one of the keys to making it work is finding underwater cover or structure bass might be using. Rarely, however, do you have to let the lure fall deeper than 12 to 15 feet to catch fish; if they're there, they'll hit.

Don't confuse slow rolling with "dropping" a spinnerbait, because they're different techniques and use different lures. By dropping a spinnerbait, we're generally talking about fishing the lure nearly vertically along bluffs and into creek channels. Bill Dance has made the technique popular by using it to catch fine stringers of smallmouth. Most of the time, Bill and other pros use a short-arm spinnerbait for this, the short arm being the blade arm. Instead of extending to the hook as in a "long-arm" spinnerbait, a short-arm is only half as long. Normally, it has only one blade, such as a size 3 or 4 Colorado.

Short-arm spinnerbaits are not nearly as weedless as the long-arm models, which is why we don't use them around brush. They also do not have the vibration of long-arm models, which is why they're usually fished with a large blade.

NEW SKIRT MATERIALS

One of the most dramatic changes we've seen in spinnerbaits in recent years is the development of new skirt materials. Originally, skirts were made of vinyl plastic. These produced some action in the water but if you left them in your tacklebox in the heat, they'd turn into a gooey mess. Rubber skirts were next, and were a huge improvement because they could withstand hotter temperatures and produced better action. Then in 1986, silicone became the top choice, and today the top skirt manufacturer in the United States is RM Engineering in Charleston, South Carolina. They supply skirts for nearly all the leading spinnerbait manufacturers.

I've been using spinnerbaits for more than three decades, and I'm still learning new things about them.

Spinnerbait skirts today include what is commonly known as glitter or metalflake, the flashy particles that reflect light and totally change the appearance of the skirt underwater. This glitter is produced in a sheet-like film, then chopped into its salt-and-pepper consistency and mixed with the silicone; it isn't added later. When used in spinnerbait skirts, the light reflects off the glitter to produce a more natural appearance. They allow you to actually slow down your retrieve in clear water—in effect, these skirts have turned spinnerbaits into more of a visual attraction lure for the first time in their history.

When I had my aquarium bass, I noticed that whenever a bass sucked in a minnow, the first thing it did was scale it. The bass exhaled a mass of scales through its gills and this instantly attracted other bass in the aquarium. I think when you retrieve one of these glitter skirts and stop it for a second so the skirt can open and close several times, it may look like a bass is blowing out scales. I know I've caught more bass in clear water using these skirts than I ever have before.

Because glitter skirts have made spinnerbaits more of a visually attractive lure, manufacturers have continued the progression by painting the blades and also color coordinating the head color. The end result is a complete spinnerbait that matches a bluegill, shad, or some other baitfish. The better these colors become, the more important I think they are. Even in murky water or at night, the little pieces of glitter will catch light and help make the lure more visually attractive.

Another thing you'll notice about the colored spinnerbaits is how much better you can see them underwater. You'll work cover more effectively, and even see more bass hitting. I really recommend that any spinnerbait angler study these new lures and evaluate the colors carefully.

One of the things I have always tried to use in the spinnerbaits I've designed over the years has been a thinner wire. For the industry as a whole, .035 to .045 gauge has been the standard, but I like a thinner gauge. It vibrates better. Not only do the blades vibrate, but so does the rest of the lure! Gradually, the industry is changing to these thinner wires, often using tapered wire that offers the strength of the thicker gauge and the vibration of the thinner gauge. This is another feature you need to think of when purchasing your spinnerbaits.

ADDING TRAILERS TO SPINNERBAITS

Like nearly all bass fishermen, I add trailers to my spinnerbaits, just as I do with jigs. In cold water or when I fish a spinnerbait slow I add a pork chunk, while in warm water I often add a thin plastic trailer.

Some of the skirts I use now have two long, thin strands that extend out from the rest of the skirt and these can act as a trailer. Basically, a trailer adds action to a spinnerbait, it can add casting weight if you need it, and it presents the lure as a larger package that may attract a larger bass.

Sometimes I'll also add a trailer or "stinger" hook, especially if it seems like the bass are just nipping the spinnerbait skirt. My stinger is a short shank hook that I'll hide in the skirt itself.

Because spinnerbaits are primarily a reaction-strike lure (even though we're making them more visually attractive) I like to fish them on 20-pound-test line. Occasionally I'll use 17-pound-test and if the water is extremely clear I'll use 14, but I don't believe bass pay any attention to the line size on a fast-moving lure. Besides, I like to throw a spinnerbait into thick cover and I need the extra strength heavy line provides. If the cover is really, really thick, I'll even use 25-pound-test.

9

PROBING THE BOTTOM
WITH JIGS

If you have ever been to Sam Rayburn Reservoir in Texas, or maybe just read about it, then you've heard of the Black Forest. It's up the lake along the western shoreline just below the Highway 141 bridge, and it has a reputation for producing some of the lake's largest bass. It's where I caught one of my biggest bass ever, a 12-pound, 4-ounce fish that hit a jig in March, 1990.

This lure, generally nothing more than a hook, a leadhead, and a silicone skirt, doesn't look like much, but it really is one of the most productive of all bass lures. I can't begin to tell you how many national tournaments it has won. Unfortunately, it is not an easy lure to use, at least not until you gain confidence in it and your ability to catch fish with it.

I know several top pros who forced themselves to learn to use the lures by taking nothing else in the boat with them. Gary Klein was one of these. Early in his career, Gary realized he'd have to master the jig if he wanted to succeed in professional fishing. He went fishing many times with only jigs, which forced him to use them under a variety of conditions. Today he ranks as one of the best jig fishermen in professional angling.

THE IMPORTANCE OF "LURE AWARENESS"

The difficulty with jigs is realizing when a fish has the lure. You don't always feel that "thump" or "tap" that signals a hit so you have to watch your line for movement or learn to recognize when the lure suddenly "feels heavy" as you start to retrieve it. This is known as lure awareness, and it's something all serious and successful bass fishermen learn. It is part of the technique of fishing any free-falling lure, and it involves concentration, knowing exactly where your lure is at all times, and what it is doing in the water.

With a jig, I think one of the most crucial parts of learning how to fish this way is choosing the correct weight, because a jig's weight largely determines its rate of fall. The lighter the jig, the slower it falls.

Normally, a slow, steady fall is the most productive day in and day out, but there are many times—such as in heavy brush or vegetation—where a light jig won't penetrate that cover, so you have to use a heavier one.

A jig's weight determines how fast the lure will fall, but you can slow the lure by using a larger pork or plastic trailer, or speed it up by using a smaller one. Using heavy line will also slow a jig.

The depth of the water you're fishing also needs to be considered when you're choosing jig weight. The more shallow you're fishing, the lighter jig you need, and remember to try to get a slow fall.

Among the bass tournament pros, the favorite jig weights are ⅜ and ½ ounce, but I will use jigs as light as ¼ ounce and as heavy as a full ounce. In clear water or very shallow water, I'll use a lighter ¼-ounce jig down to a depth of about four or five feet, and work it with 12-pound-test line. In extremely heavy vegetation like the grass beds on Rayburn or Toledo Bend, or Lake Murray in South Carolina, I'll use heavier ¾- and one-ounce jigs because I want them to penetrate the vegetation and reach the open water underneath. Here I'll also use 25- or even 30-pound-test line.

Other than by the weight of the jig itself, there are two primary ways you can slow down or speed up the rate of fall. These are by changing line size or trailer size. Heavy lines, such as 20-, 25-, and 30-pound-test will slow a jig's fall, as will a larger pork or plastic trailer. That's how we get a ½-ounce jig to settle slowly into a bush. We use a really heavy line and a big trailer. Sometimes, however, particularly in summer when bass may be a little more active, you may want your jig to fall faster. If this is the case, simply downsize your trailer, or change line sizes if you can get away with it.

How do you know if bass want a fast or slow falling jig? You don't. Just assume they want it slow. History proves that's what fish prefer most of the time. If however, you happen to get a bite as you're bringing your jig up on the retrieve, chances are the bass want something faster. The fish watched your lure fall slowly, then hit on the faster retrieve.

Overall, bass hit jigs most often on the fall, and this is one reason lure awareness and concentration are so important. A bass can easily suck in your jig without you ever feeling anything!

LEARN TO WATCH THE LINE

The way you overcome this is by watching your line at the point where it enters the water. If a bass hits, you'll see the line twitch slightly, or if it's a big hit, the line will actually jump. Learning to do this is crucial because many bites do come on the initial fall, and this is when you have the least control of the jig.

I probably don't feel 50 percent of the strikes I get on a jig, but I see them because I am a line watcher. I use clear Stren, not a florescent line, because I can see it well but the bass don't seem to pay any attention to it.

HOPPING THE JIG

There are dozens of ways to work a jig, but I prefer to use short hops rather than crawling it slowly along the bottom. I let it settle to the bottom, then give it one short hop, let it settle again, then hop it another time. Each hop probably moves

One of the most important aspects of jig fishing is learning to watch your line to determine strikes. Bass tend to hit jigs as they fall, so picking up strikes requires concentration.

the lure only four or five inches and I do this only three or four times. If I haven't gotten a strike by then, I reel in for another pitch to a new target.

I developed this retrieve after watching bass react to crawfish in my aquarium. The crawfish would settle right to the bottom, then immediately raise its pinchers in a defensive position as a bass approached. In practically every instance the bass would stop a few inches away to watch the crawfish, which wouldn't move. You'd think the fish was losing interest until suddenly it would just suck the crawfish in like a vacuum cleaner.

Hopping the jig also accomplishes something else. It helps you establish a rhythm in working the lure and makes strikes easier to detect.

When you hop a jig, it should feel the same way each time, and when it doesn't you need to set the hook. In contrast, crawling a jig along the bottom feels different every time, since you're moving over different objects. Until you're really familiar and comfortable with a jig, you'll have trouble realizing when you have a strike.

RAISING THE ROD AND SHAKING

Another retrieve variation is raising your rod tip and shaking the jig. This can be effective when fishing brushy cover and your line drops over a limb or branch. Lower the jig to the bottom, then raise it a few inches and shake it, then lower it. Then raise it and shake it another time. This will also help you establish a rhythm and allow you to better detect strikes.

Normally, I use a jig when I'm fishing specific, visible cover, and I make my first presentation right where I believe the bass is going to be. This can be in the very center of a bush, beside a piling, or behind a rock. I don't spend time around the outside of the cover first and gradually work my lure in; I don't want to take a chance of spooking the fish nor do I want to give a bass a lot of chances to look at the bait.

I want a reflex strike, which a jig seems to get much of the time. That's one reason it's such an excellent big-bass lure. It represents an easy-to-grab prey a bass doesn't have to expend much energy to get. At the same time, jigs are perhaps the very best lures we have to present in the thick heavy cover where big bass live.

SWIMMING JIGS

Some fishermen like to swim jigs. To me, this is like slow rolling a spinnerbait. The lure is crawled slowly but steadily over every log, stick, or clump of grass along the bottom. Why use a jig instead of a spinnerbait to fish this way? The only real reason I can think of is because you like fishing jigs more than spinnerbaits; both can be extremely effective.

You can also swim jigs over the top of submerged grass, just touching the top of the vegetation as you retrieve with slow, upward pulls of the rod tip. This is some of the hardest fishing I know, and I try to keep from having to do it whenever I can. If bass are holding over the top of deep grass, I'll use a lipless crankbait, spinnerbait, or jerk bait to try to catch them before I resort to a jig; I just don't believe this is a very efficient way to use the lure.

Texas pro Tommy Martin, a former guide on Toledo Bend, helped pioneer the technique of fishing heavy jigs through thick vegetation. In the spring, of course, jigs are excellent lure choices to hop around shoreline vegetation, but in the summer when hydrilla mats on the surface, Martin and other Texas fishermen started dropping jigs into the vegetation further offshore. They started doing this because Martin swam under the vegetation one day and discovered it was open down below, and that bass were present. All that was needed was to get a lure through two or three feet of greenery and it would fall into open, practically untouched water. This required a heavy lure, and a favorite quickly became a 1-ounce, green and white lure known as the "Toledo jig." Today jigs and large plastic worms are both used in the technique.

I have fished this way, and it's fun. Usually a short pitch-cast is the most effective presentation. You aim for the open potholes or any place the vegetation looks a little thinner, then jiggle your rod tip until the lure slips through. Then depending on where the bass are, you can jiggle your lure as it falls to the bottom, or let it drop completely to the bottom and then shake it there.

Fishing heavy vegetation like this with a jig is a special application for summer fishing, but it certainly isn't the only way you can fish jigs in warm weather. For many years, we considered jigs only for wintertime fishing, but in truth, a jig is a year-round lure. It is certainly a primary choice for cold water, but you should remember jigs at other times as well.

JIGS FOR ALL SEASONS

In warm weather a jig is good lure to use along shallow channel banks where both cover and deeper water are present. Often a crankbait or slow rolling spinnerbait will bring strikes in these situations, but it's also a good time and place for a jig. Generally, the most productive technique is to keep your boat in the middle of the deeper channel and cast to the shallow bank, slowly working your lure over the edge. You can try a hopping retrieve here as well as shaking, but remember to concentrate on cover, too, such as stumps and rocks.

Jigs will also catch suspended bass along faces of steep bluffs in all seasons. Depending on the water depth and formation of the rock below the surface, you will often do better making casts parallel to the rock face rather than straight into it. As your jig hits the water and begins falling, keep your reel in freespool so you can feed line to it.

This permits the jig to fall straight rather than in a long curving arc, and it will stay in the potential strike zone longer. It's also when you have very little control over the lure, so pay attention to your line. Bass along bluffs are nearly always suspended, which means they're going to hit the jig when it falls. You have to be ready when they do.

Jigs catch more than largemouth bass. Here a hefty six-pound smallmouth gets lifted into the boat after it hit a jig. Jigs can be used year-round in both shallow and deep water.

Jigs are also great "second cast" lures. By this I mean casting back to a spot when a bass has just struck but missed one of your other lures, such as a buzzbait or other topwater lure. If you have a jig tied on and ready, you can very often catch that fish with a quick cast to that same spot. Plastic worms also work well for this.

SOUND, COLOR, AND DESIGN TO ATTRACT BASS

The hottest jig in bass fishing today is one with rattles. I added my own rattles to jigs years ago, but now virtually every manufacturer builds them into their lures. The idea is that sound adds another way of attracting bass, and because sound travels much faster in water than in air, it's probably true. I do know bass seem to hit the sound-producing jigs better than the silent ones.

In addition to fishing jigs with rattles, very few anglers ever fish jigs without pork or plastic trailers on them. I prefer to use plastic trailers whenever the water temperature is above about 60 degrees, and pork trailers in water temperatures below that. The plastic seems to produce better overall swimming action, particularly with imitation crawfish and craw-worms, which is what the bass like in warmer water.

If you've been in any tackle stores lately, you already know jigs are made in a wide variety of styles and colors. Overall, if I were limited to a single color combination, it would be black and blue, and I believe most of the bass pros would agree with me. In spring, when crawfish tend to be more greenish yellow, I usually use a pumpkinseed color, and match my trailer with it.

I also prefer a jig with a more pointed head design. I think it comes through brush, grass, and other cover more easily. Some pros disagree with me on this, preferring instead to use a jig with a more rounded head. They say it falls slower than a jig with a pointed or angular head.

Regardless of its head design, you want to make sure that when your jig lands on the bottom, it sits head down/hook up, not flat on its side. This will allow the jig's skirt to float and billow in the water, adding to its attractiveness. You can even add little BB-sized floats to the skirt itself to help it wave in the current.

RODS FOR JIGGING

Most jig rods are fairly stiff but with a limber tip for pitching or flipping. Pitching is my preferred method of presenting a jig, so I use a 7½-foot medium/heavy rod. I use this same rod for flipping, Carolina rigs, and even deep crankbaits.

Like jigs, you should use several different models to decide which you like best for your style of fishing. Some prefer slightly shorter rods, and you may decide you actually want two different jigs rods, a more limber one for pitching and a stiffer one for vertical jigging.

Try different jig designs too, until you find one you have confidence in using. There are a lot of different designs available, but nearly all of them do the same thing, which is catch a lot of bass.

10

PLAYING WITH PLASTICS

For more than 40 years, ever since Nick Creme began making the first commercial plastic worms in the early 1950s, bass anglers have been enjoying a bounty unmatched by any other lure in history. No lure has fooled as many bass as the plastic worm.

Today the plastic worm is only part of an entire family of soft plastics available to fishermen. There are lizards, tube jigs, grubs, jerk baits, centipedes, and more. And all of them are usually available in a kaleidoscope of sizes and colors.

With the variety of lures has come a corresponding variety of techniques in using them. In professional fishing, using a lizard on a Carolina rig is unquestionably the most popular fishing method to come along in years. Plastic worms are frequently used as topwater lures now, and the hollow, squidlike tube jigs have become standard fare for springtime bedding bass.

I remember the first plastic worms I ever saw. They came pre-rigged, with either two or three hooks, several small beads, and a tiny propeller, all on a monofilament leader. Soon after, plain worms without these extras became available, and that's when bass fishermen really started experimenting with new fishing techniques.

TEXAS RIG

One of the new techniques became known as the Texas rig, and although it is quite possible several anglers in various parts of the country developed it simultaneously, many feel the Texas rig might have been started by Robert Carey Scott, of Tyler, Texas, in the mid-1960s. Scott was at least certainly one of the first to publicize it, in the June 1966 issue of *Field & Stream* magazine.

The Texas rig basically consists of a hook imbedded in the worm to make it weedless. Weight is added with a sliding sinker threaded on the line ahead of the worm. Although Scott does not specifically mention this sliding sinker in his 1966 story, he does detail how to rig the hook to make the worm weedless.

MAKING A TEXAS RIG

Basically, here's how you can make a Texas rig. Thread your line through the sinker (we use bullet-shaped sinkers, so thread the sinker on so the nose or "bullet" end faces your rod tip). Next, tie on your hook.

Since its introduction in the early 1950s, the plastic worm has probably caught more bass than any other lure. Today the entire family of soft plastics includes a wide selection of different lures.

To rig the worm weedless, insert the point of the hook into the top of the worm and pull it out ¼ to ½ inch down the worm's body. Pull the hook down until the eye is actually buried in the worm head. Now rotate the hook so the barb faces the worm body and insert the barb—not where it touches the worm but slightly further down where the curve of the hook would touch the worm. This will ensure the worm is straight.

Although I fished the Texas rig many years, I now use a slightly different sinker arrangement. The sinker I use was developed in the mid-1980s by Florida fisherman Dennis Pixton and it features a small corkscrew on its base that screws into the head of the worm. Originally known as the Pixton rig, the sinker is now sold by Gambler Lure Company in Florida.

I thread the sinker on my line, then tie on a hook. I rig the worm itself just like I've described above, with the hook imbedded in the body of the worm to make it weedless. Then I slide the sinker down and screw it firmly into the worm. This gives me a continuous worm/ sinker arrangement, which is what I want.

BENEFITS OF AN ATTACHED SINKER

My favorite presentation with a worm is pitching, rather than casting or flipping to heavy cover. I don't want a sinker sliding down the line ahead of the worm and tangling on a limb or maybe even alerting a bass. With the sinker attached, the worm falls as one unit and doesn't get snagged.

This is also important when fishing in heavy vegetation like milfoil or hydrilla, too. In fact, many fishermen "peg" their slip sinkers to their lines with slivers of toothpicks when worm fishing in vegetation, but this can damage your line. My screw-in sinker never bothers my line.

The Texas rig or the pegged sinker rig I use is most effective when fishing shallow (generally visible) cover like boathouses because it can be cast easily and accurately. There are an endless variety of retrieves possible, but I like to work a worm much the same way I work a jig—with short hops right around the cover. The majority of strikes will be within a few feet of that cover.

Just as in jig fishing, many worm strikes occur as the lure is falling so it's important to be a line watcher. One trick I try to practice is to keep my worm falling as much as possible, which is why I like to hop or jig the worm. As soon as it touches bottom, I raise my rod tip so the lure can then fall again.

SLIDER RIGS

Another light tackle worm rig known as the Slider is very popular among the pros. Developed years ago by the late Charlie Brewer of Lawrenceburg, Tennessee, a Slider basically consists of a 4-inch plastic worm with a specially designed flat head weighted hook. This flat head allows the worm to swim or "slide" through the water or over cover with a very natural appearance.

To many, Brewer is considered the father of light tackle worm fishing, as his lures are rarely fished with lines stronger than 8-pound-test. Brewer himself has caught 6- and 7-pound smallmouth on his Sliders using 4-pound-test mono.

CRAWLING PLASTIC WORMS

Crawling plastic worms along the bottom is another productive technique, although this is where I see many fishermen, especially inexperienced ones, get into trouble. They can't distinguish between a bass bite and a log "bite." Experience is

One of the pioneers in plastic worm design is Tom Mann of Eufaula, Alabama, who taught many fishermen the effectiveness of the Texas rig. Tom successfully competed in national tournaments for years.

the best teacher, of course, but my philosophy is that whenever I'm not sure what's on my line, I set the hook, and that's what I suggest to all new anglers.

If it's any consolation, I can report to you that even the most experienced fishermen miss worm strikes. In fact, underwater film studies show that some of the nation's best worm fishermen probably never feel as many as a third of the worm bites they get! That's why plastic worm fishing takes concentration and line watching.

A STARTING POINT

When you are getting started as a worm fisherman, there are always four primary variables you need to consider. These are sinker size, worm size, hook size, and worm color.

In the beginning, I suggest using a ³⁄₁₆-ounce slip sinker, a 6-inch plastic worm, and a 2/0 hook. Concerning color, try either a purple or grape worm, or a black worm with a blue tail. This is a basic starting point that will catch fish, and a combination I use very often.

Various weather and water conditions can change this combination. If I'm after larger bass, for example, I use a larger worm. I like to fish 10-inch worms, and some pros use 12 inchers! These, of course, require larger 4/0 or 5/0 hooks and a slightly heavier sinker, but you can fish them the very same way—hopping, crawling, or even swimming them around cover.

SPLIT-SHOTTING

In bad weather or in extremely clear water, when bass will probably be finicky, you'll often do better with a shorter worm, which in turn will mean a lighter sinker and a smaller hook. You'll also have to change your presentation, fishing the lure much slower and working it even tighter in cover.

When fishing conditions become extremely difficult, we sometimes resort to a technique known as split-shotting. Developed by bass fishermen in the western states, this is essentially a light line/small worm and clear water technique in which a BB-sized lead (or smaller) weight is clamped on the line about 12 inches above your worm and hook.

Personally, I don't care much for split-shotting. I don't like light line fishing that much, and I'm not convinced split-shotting actually offers that much of an advantage. In tough, clear water conditions, I look instead for dingy water and cover, and use a smaller pegged sinker worm or a jig.

One time a split-shot does seem to offer some advantages is when swimming a worm over submerged vegetation. The light weight takes the worm down but isn't heavy enough to sink it into the vegetation. Because the weight is clamped on the line, it is away from the lure so you can get good swimming action.

FLOATING WORMS

Sometimes, when I'm fishing shoreline vegetation or swimming a worm on the surface, I won't use any weight at all. Instead, I tie my fishing line to a swivel, then use a 12-inch leader from the swivel to my plastic worm. This eliminates line twist.

This floating or swimming worm has been a surprise lure in professional bass fishing for several years, and is an excellent choice for finding bass along brushy, wooded shorelines. On Lake Norman near my home, it's practically the only lure some fishermen use. It isn't a technique developed by tournament anglers however.

A good place to fish plastic worms as well as plastic tube jigs is around boat docks and piers. Here a fisherman uses a tube jig to probe brush piles along the edge of a pier.

More than 20 years ago, when Currituck Sound on the North Carolina Outer Banks was such a tremendous bass fishery, anglers there fished floating worms over the top of the vegetation and caught huge stringers of fish. The Currituck anglers did not use a leader, but instead put the swivel directly ahead of the hook, again to eliminate line twist as the worm rolled.

Topwater worm fishing is an excellent tactic for spring and summer bass holding in and around vegetation. Favorite retrieves I've had success using include short jerks that cause the worm to dart side to side erratically, and a slow, steady swimming action that causes the worm to look more like a snake.

WACKY WORMS

A slight variation of this is known as the Wacky Worm, and I first learned of it on Toledo Bend in the mid-1980s. Guides there used a straight 6-inch worm and a 1/0 hook they inserted through the middle of the worm. You can imagine the wobbling action this had when retrieved over the grass—both ends of the worm gyrated.

Because the Wacky Worm was difficult to cast, the guides began adding weight by cutting the head off a roofing nail and inserting this in one end of the worm. Bass fishermen still use this technique and today one company even markets a lure named the Whacky Worm.

TOPWATER WORM DESIGNS

Surprisingly, the three most popular colors for topwater worms are pink, yellow, and white—not colors we ever use for Texas rigs. The reason is not because the bass like them, but because these colors are the easiest for fishermen to see! Strikes on topwater worms are often very subtle, in which the fish just sucks the lure in with hardly a ripple.

In 1973, a French lure company introduced a new plastic lure design named the 'Sosy Eel' at the American Fishing Tackle Manufacturers Association show in Chicago. What set this lure apart was the fact the lure featured a curving, sickle-like tail that vibrated as the lure was retrieved.

It took only a few weeks before America's plastic worm makers incorporated the basic design into their own products, but at least one enterprising angler had already been using a swimming tail design since 1967. That man was Jim Bagley, who became far better known in the years ahead for his wood crankbaits.

Bagley's worm was named the Spring Tail, and was formed by removing still-hot plastic worms from the mold and wrapping them around a piece of balsa dowel until they cooled.

"SWIMMING TAILS" NOW A STANDARD DESIGN

Regardless of who or how the swimming tail design began, it created a revolution in soft plastic worms, and today the design is standard in every manufacturer's line. The advantage, of course, is that a swimming tail gives a worm its own built-in action. Straight-tail worms have no action of their own.

Even before Bagley began wrapping his hot worms around a piece of dowel, another bass fisherman/lure manufacturer was experimenting with other ways to give plastic worms more action. He was Lloyd Deaver of Gastonia, North Carolina, and he's the man most give credit to for developing the Carolina rig.

CAROLINA RIGS

Deaver developed a 4-inch plastic worm known as the Fish Finder, and he sold it rigged with two small hooks, similar to the way Creme first sold his worms. Initially, Deaver put a split-shot on his line for casting weight, but then he began experimenting with a heavier sinker and a swivel arrangement. With a heavier sinker, stopped some distance ahead of the worm by the swivel, Deaver was able to give his stubby little worm more jumping, darting action simply by the way he moved his rod tip.

Deaver's technique did not draw much attention from the bass pros until the 1985 Bass Masters Classic when Jack Chancellor used it to win on the Arkansas River. I was really surprised, because I'd used the Carolina rig many times over the years, as Deaver's shop in Gastonia was only a short distance from my home in Cherryville.

Today you would be hard-pressed to find a tournament pro who doesn't have a Carolina rig rod in his boat. The technique allows us to fish relatively deep water very fast. It is an excellent tool for locating bass, even in shallow water, and it will attract both big bass as well as numbers of bass.

It's better than a crankbait because you can keep it in a strike zone longer, and it's easier than a jig because you can feel it better. In vegetation it doesn't get snagged as much.

I fish a Carolina rig down to about 25 feet, and I especially like it in the summer months when bass move off the flats and into the channels. I think it may actually "call" bass to it because of the vibrations it produces.

MAKING A CAROLINA RIG

The basic Carolina rig consists of a 1-ounce bullet slip sinker, a swivel, a hook, and soft plastic lure, usually a 6- or 7-inch lizard. Thread the sinker on your line just as you would with a Texas rig, then tie the line to one terminal of your swivel. Next, tie a 3- to 4-foot leader to the other swivel terminal, then tie the other end of the leader to a 4/0 hook. Insert the hook into the lizard just like a worm, burying the barb so the lure is weedless.

WATER CONDITIONS A FACTOR

There are numerous variations of this, of course, and, as with the Texas rig, the

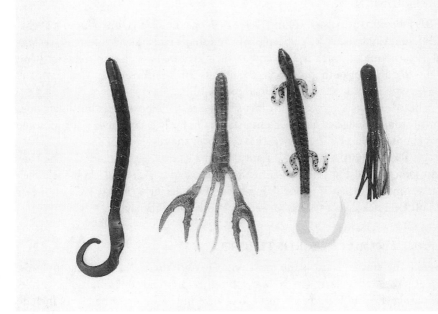

The family of soft plastic lures includes more than just worms. From left to right: worms come in a range of sizes with a variety of active tails; crawfish can be fished alone or as trailers; lizards work well with Carolina rigs; and tube jigs are popular for spring fishing.

variations usually depend on water conditions. For example, a Carolina rig is most effective in relatively open water. If you're fishing heavy cover like stumps or rocks, or if you're fishing extremely murky water, you should use a shorter leader of about 2½ feet.

In clear water, stay with a leader of 3 to 4 feet, but if you're fishing submerged vegetation, consider a 5- to 6-foot leader.

Your sinker weight is not really important except when fishing heavy grass. Even in shallow water, I still use a ¾- or 1-ounce sinker, but in thick grass I use a ½-ounce or perhaps even a lighter sinker. A heavy sinker is more difficult to pull through the grass and deadens my sense of feel for a strike. I can keep a lighter sinker, and thus my lure, above the vegetation.

Most fishermen who fish Carolina rigs generally use 17- or 20-pound-test line on their reels, then drop down a size or two, such as to 17- or 14-pound-test line, for their leaders. The reason for using a lighter leader is that if the lure gets snagged, only the leader will break and you lose just a hook and a lizard. I usually pre-rig several leaders and keep them in my boat so if I do break one, it won't take as long to retie.

SINKER DESIGN

In 1994 a company named Cajun Tackle in Tioga, Louisiana, introduced a slightly different sinker design I've been using and that I really like. It's a small, rectangular bar about a ¼-inch square and an inch long but with a slight kink or bend in the middle. On both ends there are eyelets for line threading. This company also has special rattles that also thread on your line.

The advantage I've seen with this sinker design is how well the sinker does come through obstacles like rocks and sticks. On fairly clean gravel bottom, some pros choose a round barrel swivel that rolls over the rocks easier.

We also add rattles or beads to our Carolina rigs to help attract fish. The constant knocking of the sinker against these beads adds a distinct click-click-click that at times may be the factor that makes a bass decide to strike. We put one or two of these beads on the line between the sinker and the swivel.

PLASTIC LIZARD, CHOICE OF THE PRO

Overall, the plastic lizard is the most popular Carolina rig lure among the pros. You don't see many lizards in the water, but this lure sends out vibrations with its swimming tail and legs, and it just looks alive in the water. Other lures include plastic worms, grubs, tube jigs, and even hard plastic lures like lipless crankbaits.

When the sinker is sitting still on the bottom, the lure tends to float slightly above the bottom, but as you move your rod tip, the lure begins a very erratic darting, diving action to the bottom. It can't help but attract bass.

In very muddy water, you may find bass are biting your sinker rather than your lure. If this is happening, tie a short 3- to 4-inch leader on the same terminal (you can also use a three-terminal swivel) with a small plastic grub or worm, and you'll be surprised at how many bass you catch on this lure. You have to keep the leader extremely short so it won't wind around the longer leader when you cast.

Your retrieve with a Carolina rig can be hops, jumps, crawls, or whatever you want it to be. Let the bass tell you. The key is to move the lure with your rod, not your reel. Raise and lower your rod tip rapidly to make the lure jump and hop, or sweep it slowly to one side to make the lure crawl.

SETTING THE HOOK

A Carolina rig hook-set isn't the same as with a Texas rig. With the Texas rig, when you feel a fish, lower your rod just slightly, then snap upward hard and fast. Don't worry about lowering your rod, reeling in slack, pointing at the bass, feeling to see if it's still there, and then trying to set the hook. Just lower your rod tip slightly—the slack line will let you generate rod speed—and snap your wrists upward.

With a Carolina rig, half the time you don't even need to set the hook because bass hook themselves. If you do set the hook, a fast but steady sweep to one side is usually the most effective. Just keep tension on the line and keep reeling.

CASTING THE RIGS

When you're fishing a Carolina rig, don't use anything shorter than a 6½-foot rod, because you're not really casting, you're lobbing the lure. With a long leader, it's an unwieldy lure to throw, but it is easier with a longer rod. I use a 7½ footer.

This casting, or lobbing, means you aren't going to have the same degree of accuracy you'll have with a Texas rig. That's why the Texas rig worm is best when you're fishing specific targets. The Carolina rig is primarily for more open or deeper water.

TUBE JIGS IN THE SPRING

In the spring when bass are on beds, one of the favorite lures is a tube jig. This is like a thick, round plastic worm about 4 inches long, except it's hollow and it usually has a tail of squidlike strands of plastic.

Tube jigs are fished on very light lines testing less than 10 pounds and are rigged several ways. Some rig them Texas style with a tiny slip sinker, while others use weighted leadhead hooks. They can be fished weedless or with the hook exposed.

Because they are hollow, tube jigs sink very erratically, and this is what makes them so appealing to bass. Anglers like to cast them into the nests of bedding bass, or hop them ahead of cruising bass. Either way, they're extremely effective lures for those who take the time to learn how to use them.

CRAWFISH AND CRAW-WORM PLASTICS

There are also a lot of plastic imitation crawfish or craw-worms available that are rigged the same way, either with a slip sinker or with a leadhead hook. Various sizes are available, so you can use them with both light spinning gear and heavier baitcasting tackle.

On Sam Rayburn Reservoir, Texas-rigged craw-worms fished just like plastic worms have caught some huge fish in the 13-pound class, while the smaller craw-fish imitations have been instrumental in numerous national tournament wins. Some pros like to use these crawfish as trailers for their jigs, which is just another example of how effective the entire family of soft plastics really is.

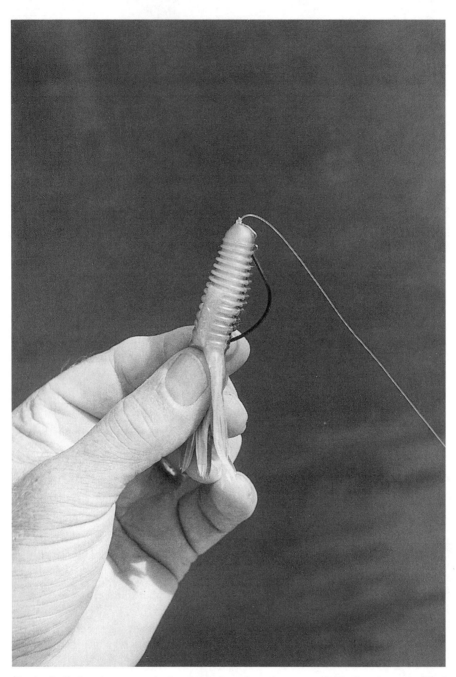

Plastic tube jigs have become popular because the larger lures sizes now available allow them to be fished with heavier tackle. I like to rig tube jigs weedless so I can flip them into thick brush.

11

POWER FISHING WITH PLASTIC TUBES

If ever professional bass fishermen have had a "secret" lure, I'd say it would be the oversized plastic tube jig. Between about 1992 and 1997, a group of pros, including Doug Garrett, Larry Nixon, George Cochran, and Scott Rook, played a major role in developing and perfecting a technique of power fishing that has since become a widely practiced tactic in tournament competition.

"Power" fishing is a term we use to describe how we use larger, heavier tackle to fish larger, fast-moving lures like spinnerbaits, crankbaits, and even jigs. The opposite of power fishing is "finesse" fishing, which employs the use of smaller, slower-moving lures with light lines. We finesse fish in clear water or whenever bass are really inactive.

Doug and the other pros figured out a way to combine these two techniques, using a tube jig originally designed for finesse fishing with heavier line and tackle more common with power fishing. It's not quite as simple as it sounds, believe me, and it took them several years to really perfect the method.

TUBE JIG DEVELOPMENT

Remember, Doug didn't invent the tube lure, or tube jig as we commonly call it today. Two Arizona experts, Bobby and Gary Garland, developed the first ones back in 1975, naming their product the Gitzit. A tube lure is like a short plastic worm or grub, except that it's hollow, just like a tube, and the tail is cut into a lot of thin strands like a squid. The first tubes were fairly thin, only about 2½ inches long, and used primarily with ultralight weights and very light lines in clear water. In short, they were—and still are—great finesse lures.

Garrett, who had been a long-time Gitzit fisherman but who also liked the power fishing techniques of pitching and flipping big jigs and worms into thick cover, developed a larger-than-normal tube jig so he could rig it Texas style with a slip sinker, a 4/0 wide gap hook, and 20-pound-test line. It took a larger tube to handle this size weight, hook, and line—up to 4½ inches long and both fatter and thicker. But once he started flipping them into the thickest, heaviest cover he could find and catching a lot of bass, he knew he was on to something, and he only told a few of his closest Arkansas fishing friends about it.

SPREADING THE WORD

Fortunately for all of us, Doug let the cat out of the bag when he won the 1997 B.A.S.S. MegaBucks tournament and an outdoor writer cornered him about it. The technique gained even more exposure and credibility when Denny Brauer won the 1998 Bass Masters Classic pitching and flipping a big tube jig.

The Garland tubes were primarily fished with an exposed hook, too, in open water. The lure's appeal came from its hollow design, which caused it to flutter slowly and erratically through the water rather than sinking straight to the bottom like a standard jig. The tube could also be hopped and even retrieved in a swimming motion, which caused the tentacle-like strands to wave and undulate, and it could be also worked in current, letting water flow wash and bounce it downstream like a natural food morsel. Garrett's larger tubes could be also be fished this way, but it was the technique of flipping them on heavy line that the pros really liked.

Given a choice, I believe most of us prefer power fishing. We're generally more comfortable with baitcasting reels than spinning reels, and, as a rule, power fishing is much faster. Even flipping can be done quickly.

Doug showed his oversized tube jigs to another friend of mine, Scott Rook, who began using them very successfully along the Arkansas River near his home in Little Rock, and Scott told Larry Nixon and George Cochran about them. George, in fact, even managed to use the lures part of the time in winning the 1996 Bass Masters Classic without anyone learning the secret.

Today, these larger, stronger tube lures are made and distributed by a lot of companies, including Pradco, Strike King, Mizmo, and Lake Fork Tackle. Sizes range from 3½ to as long as 5 inches in length, and many of them have solid heads, which allows for the use of larger hooks and also makes them more durable. You can flip or pitch these lures into the very places big bass usually live, and chances are, it's a lure they probably haven't seen before.

I really became interested in using tube jigs for power fishing shortly after Doug's MegaBucks win. I believe the lure has some obvious advantages over normal jig and plastic worm fishing that are worth considering.

ADVANTAGES OF A TUBE JIG

First, a tube has more action than a regular jig, due to its design. Without a wavy trailer, when a jig falls, all it does is fall. A tube sinks slower and the tail strands "swim" on the way down. Even at 4½ inches, it's still a fairly compact lure, so it will penetrate brush fairly easily.

Secondly, and probably the main reason I like a plastic tube lure is because it's more versatile than a jig. In addition to pitching and flipping, you can skip it underneath overhanging cover like drooping willow branches or a boat dock wall. You can fish a tube on a Carolina rig, you can split-shot it, and you can even

Pitching or flipping tube jigs to boat docks are favorite techniques because bass frequently use the docks for shade and cover. With spinning tackle, the tubes can even be skipped underneath the docks.

drop-shot it. By holding your rod tip up and reeling fast, you can even skip or "jump" the tube back to you as a topwater lure, making it appear like a fleeing baitfish.

RIGGING A TUBE JIG

One of the things I really like to do with a tube, especially when I know I'm around schooling bass, is attach an Eaker Shaker blade in front of the lure. This small cupped blade, which is smaller than a fingernail, acts like a bulldozer and pushes water so the lure really jumps. I developed these several years ago, and am proud to say anglers all over the country are using them both on tubes and floating worms to add more surface commotion.

When I Texas rig a plastic tube, I use a 3/0 Eagle Claw HP wide-gap hook with the 3 ½ inch tubes, and a slightly larger 4/0 hook with the 4½ inch tubes. You need a wide-gap hook to insure good hooking power after the hook penetrates the fatter body of the tube. I use either a ³⁄₁₆- or a ¼-ounce sinker too. In heavy, heavy cover, I usually use one of the Gambler Screw-Loc sinkers that screws into the head of the tube, but in more open water with less cover I let the sinker slide up and down the line.

Generally speaking, I use the smaller 3½-inch tube with a spinning rod and 10- to 14-pound-test line, and fish around rocks and outside cover. This size tube lure is really good when the water is still cold in early spring and the bass may not be as active. When I'm pitching to heavier cover, I always use a larger 4½-inch tube and my pitching rod with 20-pound-test line.

One of the first times I fished a tube lure was on Lake St. Clair near Detroit. Up there I used a hook with a weighted ¼-ounce head, a type of jighead rather than a sliding sinker. All I did was make a long cast and let the tube sink to the bottom about 20 feet down. Then I'd just drag the bait along the bottom as the wind blew my boat across the water. It worked great for St. Clair's smallmouth bass, and it could hardly have been easier. I'm sure you could use this same technique practically anywhere you fished a clear, open bottom.

DROP-SHOT RIG

The drop-shot rig is absolutely one of the neatest fishing techniques I've ever tried, and it will also work wherever you fish a fairly clear bottom. It's a type of reverse split-shot rig. Basically, just tie your sinker at the end of your line. Don't use a bullet weight; instead, just a round ball sinker. Now, about 12 inches above the sinker, tie on your hook using a simple Palomar or figure-eight knot. Thread on the tube with the hook exposed for open water or insert the hook into the wall of the tube to make it weedless for light, scattered grass or brush.

The real key here is to keep the sinker on the bottom so your lure is suspended above it. Even when bass are down deep, rarely are they holding on the absolute bottom. Instead, they're a foot or more above it, which is exactly where your drop-shot puts the tube. You can work the lure vertically over the side of the boat just by gently jigging your rod tip, or you can make short casts and actually "walk" the lure back to you by slowly raising and lowering your rod tip.

With a drop-shot like this, the lure stands almost straight out from your line, but it doesn't touch the bottom. You may never feel a strike either. Bass just sip in the lure and swim away, so you have to be a line watcher.

SPLIT-SHOT AND CAROLINA RIGS

I really like tube jigs on Carolina rigs and split-shot rigs too. With a Carolina rig, each time you jerk your rod, the tube jumps into the air, then swims and zigzags back to the bottom. I use a Carolina rig when I'm working water deeper than five feet, and I'll normally use a larger tube too. Anything more shallow than that, and I'll use a split-shot, clamping a small weight about two feet above the lure. If I'm in big-bass water, I'll use a larger sized tube but normally I'll use a smaller one, as well as downsize my line to between 10- and 14-pound-test.

WHY ARE TUBES EFFECTIVE?

One of the things that may make a tube jig more effective than a normal jig is that it might somehow generate a different type of strike reaction from the bass.

Instead of a lazy opportunistic bite that a jig might bring, I think a tube lure actually creates more of a feeding reaction strike. This is only a guess, but for whatever reason, bass definitely see a tube differently than a jig.

After Denny Brauer won the 1998 Bass Masters Classic, he told me he had actually located the bass he caught with a jig during practice, but once the tournament began, those bass simply stopped hitting the lure. Here was one of the world's best jig fishermen who could not catch a fish on a jig. So Denny switched to the tube lure. He flipped it into the exact same shallow, laydown trees, and actually had bass chasing the lure trying to eat it.

That's a pretty strong endorsement for a lure, and a fishing technique, if you ask me. I'm just glad Doug, Scott, and the others decided to share their secret with the rest of us.

Your collection of crankbaits should include a variety of models that cover all the depth ranges you like to fish. You'll also want different sizes to match baitfish sizes throughout the year.

12

GETTING MORE FROM YOUR CRANKBAITS

Historically, the class of lures known as crankbaits—rounded plugs with front lips or bills to make them dive—dates back nearly a century, but as far as bass tournament competition is concerned, crankbait history began June 22, 1972. That's the day the B.A.S.S. Tennessee Invitational began on Watts Bar Lake. More importantly, that's the day Billy Westmorland's secret lure was discovered and changed forever the world of crankbaits.

Westmorland was using a new balsa wood diving plug named the Big O, and he was catching a lot of bass with it. Carved by Fred Young and named for his brother Odis, a 6'6" football player, the lure looked like a fat, rounded minnow but featured a short, slanting bill that caused it to dive and wobble.

Before the tournament was over, Big Os were renting for $5 and selling for $25, and before the year was over, several more companies had copied the design and started marketing additional crankbaits. Development has continued ever since, and although Big Os have long since disappeared from the market, crankbaits have become some of the most popular of all bass lures.

CRANKBAITS ARE VERSATILE

I use crankbaits all year. They catch bass in warm water, cold water, clear water, dingy water, deep water, and shallow water. You can fish them on the surface or on the bottom, and with a little special rod tip trickery, you can keep them suspended at mid-depth ranges right beside a piece of cover. You can throw them right into cover too, and often bring them right out. In short, I think crankbaits are more versatile than spinnerbaits.

WATER DEPTH

The first consideration for choosing a crankbait is depth. The lures are designed in various ways so that they will achieve a certain depth, such as five feet, 10 to 12 feet, or perhaps even 20 feet. If you want to get serious about crankbaiting, you'll need a selection of lures that cover these various ranges. Most crankbait manufacturers today put this depth information on the package, but use this only as a basic reference. You can vary the actual depth a crankbait runs by as much as two feet, depending on your line size and the distance of your cast.

For example, changing from 17-pound-test line to a lighter, thinner 10-pound-test line will add more than a foot to the depth the lure dives. Your speed of retrieve will also affect the lure's depth; if you want maximum depth, reel slowly and steadily and keep your rod tip down so the angle of your line doesn't pull the lure up.

You need crankbaits that reach different depths so you can hit the bottom, or hit the cover you're fishing. In the pros, we call this "contact crankbaiting," and it's what we strive for about 90 percent of the time we're using these lures. We want the lure to make contact with the cover or structure because that's where the bass usually are.

The 10 percent of the time we don't want this usually occurs in the summer months when bass tend to suspend. Then we don't want a crankbait to dive below the fish because they won't turn down to get it. They probably won't come up for a crankbait running above them either, so you try to get one that runs right through the middle of them.

You'll notice crankbaits come in a wide selection of sizes, from as short as 1 inch to over 3 inches. I think it's important to have a selection of different sizes because another key to crankbait success is matching the lure to the size of baitfish.

At times this can be critical, but don't worry about trying to find a really small crankbait that dives to 20 feet or more because there aren't any. When you want to fish extremely deep water, the larger crankbaits are all you need.

For the most part, the depth a crankbait dives is determined by the length of its bill. Longer bills push more water aside so the lure travels deeper. This is also what makes deep-diving crankbaits so effective in shallow water—the bill helps deflect the lure over limbs and other obstacles that would otherwise snag it.

CRANKBAITS WOBBLE

Whenever anyone talks about crankbaits, you'll eventually hear the term "wobble." This is how we describe a crankbait's side-to-side vibration, and it is also determined by the lure's bill. If the bill slants downward sharply from the body, the lure will tend to have a "wide" wobble, which describes the amount the lure moves from side to side. In some lures, this can be as much as 2 inches.

On the other hand, if the crankbait bill extends straight out from the lure, the wobble will be "tight," meaning it does not move that far from side to side.

THE IMPORTANCE OF WOBBLE

Is wobble critical? Believe me, I have seen times when it truly was the deciding factor in getting bass to hit. Generally speaking, the clearer the water you're fishing, the less (tighter) wobble you want, and the more dingy or off-colored the water, the more (wider) wobble you want.

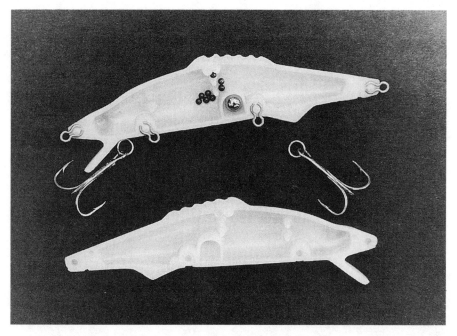

Most crankbaits today have rattles in them, usually in the form of small lead shot contained in one or more chambers in the plug body. I believe rattles help attract bass to the lure.

Wide-wobbling crankbaits work well in colder water and under conditions where bass are holding very tight to cover, such as in strong current. This is because you can work the lures slower which is how bass usually want lures presented under those conditions, and still maintain precise depth control. If you slow down a tight-wobbling crankbait, you don't get the vibration you need.

LIPLESS CRANKBAITS

There is another category of crankbaits that should also have some space in your tackle box. These are known as lipless crankbaits because they don't have a bill. Some call them vibrating swimming lures, because they have a very tight vibration or wobble and they resemble swimming minnows or baitfish.

FEELING CRANKBAITS

The greatest misconception anglers have about crankbaits is that they're simply cast-and-crank lures that soon become very boring to use. Nothing could be further from the truth. To become truly good with a crankbait, you have to learn to "feel" it just like you do a worm or jig.

My friend David Fritts, who won the 1993 Bass Masters Classic using crankbaits, is one of the best at feeling these lures, and to illustrate what feel really

Different crankbaits have different vibration or "wobble." In many instances this vibration is critical in drawing strikes from bass, so it's important that you learn to feel this vibration.

means, he tells the story of a summer tournament he fished on Lake Wylie, not far from my home.

In two days Fritts caught 14 bass weighing 57 pounds; one of his partners caught three bass, the other day's partner didn't catch any. Four of the bass Fritts caught died because they absolutely swallowed his lure, but neither of his partners ever felt the bass hit or spit out their crankbaits.

That's what feeling a crankbait is all about, and it involves more than just the lure. It also includes the line and rod you use. Essentially, you want a strong, small-diameter line with very low stretch. Low stretch translates into increased sensitivity for you to feel light strikes. Several lines like this are now available on the market.

I've already mentioned that using lighter, smaller diameter lines will allow a crankbait to run deeper, but remember also that a heavier, thicker line will keep a crankbait from running as deep as it's actually designed to go, and there are times when you may want this. In fact, this is what helped me win down at Sam Rayburn. The cold front that turned the bass so sluggish forced me to use a very slow-moving lure worked over the top of submerged vegetation. I was fishing one of the lipless crankbaits that sinks when you stop reeling so I used 20-pound-test Stren MagnaThin line to help keep the lure above the grass. That way, I could just crawl it over the top of the hydrilla.

ROD SHOULD NOT BE TOO STIFF

Your rod also needs to be either a medium- or medium/heavy-action with a general parabolic action so the entire rod bends with a bass, not just the tip. This is most critical just as you bring a bass to the boat; a rod that is too stiff will actually pull the hook from a bass if it happens to make one last surge to escape. This is one reason many pros have changed from graphite to fiberglass rods when fishing crankbaits and topwater lures. Glass rods are "slower" and tend to have a better parabolic action than most graphites.

This is a very difficult concept to understand, particularly if you're just getting started in fishing, and my advice is to try different rods and simply determine for yourself which one suits your style of fishing best.

"STAND-STILL" CRANKBAITING

Your rod also plays an important role when you work a crankbait beside brush or even through it. One of my favorite techniques for diving lures is something I call "stand-still" crankbaiting, in which I try to keep a lure right beside a bush or stump for 10 to 15 seconds to make really unaggressive bass hit. When you do this in shallow water, cast beyond your target and make the lure dive to the target by sweeping your rod hard to one side. This gets your rod in position and also takes all the slack out of your line. Keep your rod tip down and don't let any slack form in the line, because if it does, the lure will begin floating to the surface and leave the strike zone.

To keep the lure looking alive, start making short jerks with the rod tip so the lure darts forward just a couple of inches; this will also help overcome the lure's tendency to float upward. Don't make hard jerks like you do with a topwater lure, just short, quick movements. The lure will stay right beside the cover.

In water less than four feet deep, the type of crankbait I normally use for this technique is more commonly known as a jerk bait. It's a long, slender lure with a very small lip so it doesn't dive very deep but it really looks like a minnow. They're especially effective in spring when fished over shallow grassbeds.

I use the same technique in deeper water with a deeper diving crankbait and many times I actually reel my lure into the cover. The second I feel the crankbait hit anything, I stop reeling. This causes the lure to begin to float away. I use a balsa wood lure for this because it tends to float backward as it starts upward while plastic crankbaits go straight up. After a moment's pause, I reel the crankbait right into the cover again and stop the instant it makes contact. You can do this all day if you want to and never move the crankbait more than five inches, but hopefully, you won't need to keep it down there that long. Sooner or later a bass will hit if one is present.

A number of companies, including PRADCO, Norman, Bagley, and Rapala, now manufacture what are known as "suspending" lures. You simply reel them down to the desired depth, and they'll stay there, or suspend, without your having to do anything special with your rod. Storm Manufacturing even introduced some special stick-on lead weights in 1994 that can be applied (and later removed) to make any crankbait a suspending model.

When you do reel into cover, such as one of the brush piles under a boat dock or a Christmas tree someone has planted out on a point, stop reeling and raise your rod tip. Gently you can guide your crankbait through the limbs without getting snagged. Be prepared for a strike, however, as soon as you clear the brush, because this is when many of them come.

Strikes frequently occur just after crankbaits ricochet off stumps, rocks, or the bottom, which is why it's important to have a lure that reaches the bottom. Some fishermen like to stick their rod tips down into the water to gain even more depth when they're cranking but I don't like to because I think it interferes with hook-setting. Not all bass hook themselves when they hit a crankbait.

DEEP-DIVING CRANKBAITS IN SHALLOW WATER

One of the techniques that has really gained popularity in recent years among the bass pros is fishing the deep-diving crankbaits in shallow water. I've caught a lot of fish this way, and I believe one reason is because perhaps the bass haven't seen that many crankbaits in the shallows. They're more accustomed to seeing spinnerbaits or buzzbaits.

I like a long-billed crankbait for this because it helps keep the lure from getting snagged, since I'm usually fishing fallen timber, roots, stumps, and other woody cover. I have also done well crankbaiting around rock riprap and even over grass. The key is being patient because you are going to snag occasionally. Just remember to stop reeling when you hit something and then try to guide your lure through with your rod.

When you're fishing points, flats, or even shorelines, remember to vary your retrieve speed until you find something the bass want. Reel your lure down quickly, then stop, reel again, pull the rod, do anything you can think of. Surprisingly, in many lakes in the spring when bass are around underwater grass, one of the most effective retrieves is a very fast retrieve with either a diving crankbait or one of the lipless models.

DEEP CRANKING

The hardest crankbaiting of all is what is known as "deep cranking," which can be at depths as far down as 20 feet. Generally, this is when you're probing special structure like a creek channel edge, an underwater ridge, or possibly some specific cover you know is present. Being able to feel your lure when you do this is critical, because if the wobbling stops, it usually means a bass has hit. As underwater film footage has shown, however, a bass can literally suck in a crankbait with two treble hooks and spit it out without getting hooked and without you feeling anything!

A lot of deep cranking is exploratory fishing, so do as much of your homework ahead of time before you start cranking. Try to key on channel bends or abrupt shallow water/deep water combinations. Any place a channel cuts close to a shoreline, for instance, is a great location for crankbaiting. So is the mouth of a major creek where it empties into a main lake.

You can fish crankbaits around points, underneath boat docks, along steep bluff banks, and over shallow sloping coves. There's hardly anyplace you can't use a crankbait where the bass won't hit it.

13

Fun with Topwater Lures

Several years ago, another well-known tournament angler, Hank Parker, and I spent a week chasing big bass in the thick timber and swamps of Lake Marion, part of the Santee-Cooper Lakes of South Carolina. The weather was boiling hot but I don't think in all my years of bass fishing that I've ever caught, or lost, as many big fish as Hank and I did that week.

The monsters were back in the shade around logs and stumps and weeds, along the edge of a little 5-foot channel. Each time they'd strike a lure, it sounded like an alligator hitting; our lines frequently broke on the heavy cover and Hank even broke a rod!

What makes that trip so memorable is not so much the fact that we caught big bass, but rather, that we caught all our fish on topwater buzzbaits. We saw every smashing strike, and usually at very close range. To see bass strike at eye level like this is truly one of the prime attractions for using topwater lures. In extremely clear water, which is normal on some Western impoundments like Lake Mead or Lake Powell, you can see bass approaching from 20 or 30 feet deep to hit your plug, and when you do, believe me, your heart starts beating a little faster.

To be honest, however, another even better reason to use topwater lures is that some of them are true big-bass catchers. Those chattering, clattering buzzbaits Hank and I used in Lake Marion are excellent big-fish lures, as are the famous Zara Spook and the Jitterbug.

THE IMPORTANCE OF SURFACE LURES

You don't hear much about topwater lures among the bass tournament pros and because you don't, many anglers think surface lures aren't used very much. Nothing could be further from the truth. We use them a lot; in fact, there is hardly a tournament in which some type of surface lure doesn't play a role. We just don't talk much about topwater lures because unless conditions are perfect—overcast skies and calm water—the topwater bite on most lakes is pretty fragile. It doesn't last very long after daylight. Once the sun clears the horizon, we begin using other lures that will catch fish faster.

This doesn't mean topwater lures wouldn't catch bass the rest of the day, because they would. It's just that in tournament fishing, we're geared for speed. The primary ingredient needed for topwater success is patience, and most tournament pros don't have it. In truth, surface lures can be used successfully any time

Jack Wingate has caught hundreds of bass on topwater lures on Lake Seminole. He uses a certain cadence in retrieving his lures, which helps him concentrate and work the lures properly. Topwater lures will catch bass in both clear and muddy water, on both calm and windy days, and under bright and cloudy skies.

of day and practically year-round. The only time topwater action really isn't practical is when the water temperature falls below 50 degrees, but even then I've seen bass hit noisy plugs danced over shallow moss beds.

Topwater lures are primarily shallow water lures, so naturally they're most effective when bass are in shallow water. This means not only under overcast skies, but also on clear days when a breeze ripples the surface. Even on clear, calm days when bass tend to suspend and don't seem interested in crankbaits or soft plastics, they can be tempted to come up for a topwater lure.

You can also use topwater lures in high, muddy water with surprising success, and they're among the best lure choices when fishing rivers and streams where bass normally live shallow. I have used both buzzbaits and chuggers for years on the far upper portions of Lake Norman where the Catawba River has current.

TYPES OF TOPWATER LURES

The easiest way to distinguish the various types of topwater lures is to categorize them according to their designs and/or actions.

Tournament pro Gary Klein brings in a buzzbait-hooked bass while fishing a shallow stump flat on the Arkansas River. Buzzbaits usually produce the best results when fished slow and close to shallow cover.

Among the bass pros, the most common designations are "chuggers," which include such popular plugs as the Pop-R and Chug Bug; the "prop baits" or "slush baits," that include lures with propellers like the Tiny Torpedo, Woodchopper, and Devil's Horse; and the "stick baits," which include the Zara Spook, Slap-Stick, and Woodwalker.

Each of these categories of lures is designed to perform in a certain way or produce the best results under specific conditions. For example, in clear, calm water, it is usually better to fish a quiet topwater lure that doesn't cause a lot of disturbance, or, if you're using a noisy lure, to fish it slowly. A good choice might be a Zara Spook.

On the other hand, if you're fishing dingy water, the noisy chuggers with their concave faces that "pop" each time you move them, or a prop bait that churns the water, will help attract fish. Possible choices would include buzzbaits or a Pop-R.

Later in the spring and into the summer I often prefer the prop baits because I want some noise to help attract fish to the lure. This is often a good time to use buzzbaits, especially if you're after big bass. In clear, calm water, I might use a Zara Spook stick bait too.

The fall months are prime buzzbait months, because bass are moving shallow to feed. I have noticed bass frequently hit buzzbaits better this time of year if I replace the skirt with a plastic imitation shad; it's almost as if the bass are feeding by sight.

Buzzbaits will certainly catch fish in cold water too, as my friend Jim Morton proved in his win in the 1992 Bassmaster Oklahoma Invitational on Grand Lake. He had to reel it very, very slowly, but the bass were extremely shallow and they kept hitting, even after rain and a severe cold front came through the area.

Buzzbaits have been popular in tournament bass fishing since the late 1970s when they first began showing up in competition. Today, the basic design hasn't changed much. The major differences are in blade design, with some blades now having three "wings," as opposed to the standard two. Some manufacturers also have a smaller blade mounted within a larger blade, both rotating around the same shaft.

Many anglers try to tune their buzzbaits so the blade squeaks or makes noise as it rotates. Often, simple wear and tear on the lure will cause this, but I'm not totally convinced blade noise helps attract bass to a buzzbait. To me, the key in using this lure is fishing it as slowly as possible on the surface and keeping it very close to visible cover.

One of the few times I'll fish a buzzbait in deep water is around bridge abutments and pilings. In the heat of the day in the summer, bass suspend in the murky depths beside the concrete, and a buzzbait will sometimes draw frightening strikes from these fish. You never see them coming because of the dark shadows, but you certainly feel them!

FISHING WITH TOPWATER LURES

As I mentioned earlier, one of the major keys in fishing any topwater lure, including buzzbaits, is patience. Traditionally, a slow, tantalizing retrieve will be the most successful (but this is certainly not always true) and this takes time. Like other lures, it's also important to fish topwater lures as close as possible to cover, and even bump that cover occasionally.

Another key in fishing most topwater lures is to develop a cadence or rhythm when working the lure. There are an infinite number of cadences you can try, but the reason for developing one is because rod movement and reel turning must be coordinated. You have to make a topwater lure work for you, and you do it by developing this cadence.

This cadence is not for the bass, as many anglers believe. It's for you. By concentrating on the cadence, you're concentrating on working your lure properly and consistently, and that's what attracts the bass. In no other category of lures is the retrieve pattern so critical as it is with topwater plugs.

"SHAVE AND A HAIRCUT . . ."

Jack Wingate, the well-known owner of Lunker Lodge on Georgia's Lake Seminole, enjoys his topwater fishing to the tune of "shave and a haircut, six bits,"

Although some topwater lures will bring bass up from deep clear water, topwater fishing is generally better in shallow water. Anglers usually concentrate around visible cover, bumping that cover with the lure.

jerking his rod tip and making half-turns of his reel handle on cast after cast. Other anglers may have equal success with a jerk-jerk-crank, jerk-jerk-crank retrieve.

There is no exact jerking and reeling routine, and you may discover the routine that produces strikes in the morning doesn't work in the afternoon.

WALKING A SPOOK

With the exception of buzzbaits, which have to be retrieved steadily so they remain on the surface, most topwater lures work best on a slack line. This is particularly true of lures like the Zara Spook that are "walked" side to side across the water. This means that when you're holding your rod down and make a quick, jerking movement with your rod—moving the rod tip only a foot or so—you must also move the rod back to its original position. In essence, the rod acts like it's vibrating back and forth. When you jerk the rod down, the Zara Spook darts to one side and the immediate slack line is what allows it to swing back to the opposite side.

Now do you see why establishing a cadence is so important? It's to help you work the lure.

Getting a Zara Spook or one of the other stick baits to "walk" is only part of the job. Next, you have to learn how to control the speed at which it walks, because sometimes bass want it slow and other times they want it fast. How fast you can "vibrate" your rod tip determines that lure speed.

Another aspect to consider is how sharp you jerk your rod tip. A really quick jerk with little slack will keep the lure walking tighter and thereby create more surface commotion, while a slower rod movement with more slack will produce a wider walk.

If you have trouble walking a Spook, don't feel discouraged. It's one of the hardest techniques in all of bass fishing and only a very few pros I know can do it well consistently. It takes hours and hours of practice.

POPPING CHUGGERS

The category of topwater lures we call chuggers are easier to fish, and several retrieve possibilities exist. These lures attract bass by the sound they make as they are jerked or popped through the water. The concave face pushes water out and literally produces a "pop." That's why lures have been named Pop-R, Pico Pop, or P. J. Pop.

The time honored retrieve with these lures is to let the lure rest quietly on the water until the ripples subside, then, with a gentle upward jerk of your rod tip, to "pop" the lure once or twice. Then you let it sit again quietly. Pop again. Sit. Pop. Sometimes this is what it takes, and this is certainly a retrieve you need to try if bass seem to be sluggish and reluctant to hit faster retrieves.

Early morning and late afternoon are among the best times to fish topwater lures, but bass will actually hit them anytime. Topwater fishing takes patience, which many tournament pros don't have.

When the bass are more active however, you can pop these lures across the surface in a continuous retrieve, starting with your rod tip high and gradually lowering it as the lure gets closer. You can also walk them just like a Zara Spook.

MODIFYING THE POP-R

Still another retrieve is a faster variation of this, in which the lure skips over the surface like a fleeing baitfish. Zell Rowland of Texas, one of the best topwater anglers I know, has had good success using this retrieve with the Pop-R, quite possibly because he modifies them so they slide through the water easier. Zell sands the lures so they're smoother, and he also sands the face so it has a sharper edge. The difference these two simple modifications make to the lure is amazing.

A lot has been written about making a Pop-R "spit" water as it is popped. This spitting is what many anglers believe makes the lure so effective, but Zell doesn't really think so. By carefully sanding around the face, he changes the design just enough to change the sound and the spitting is simply a by-product. When you really think about it, a bass under the surface isn't paying attention to the spitting anyway.

Rowland and several other Texas anglers were largely responsible for bringing the Pop-R back on the market. It had been dropped from the Rebel (now PRADCO) catalog in 1979 because of poor sales, but some of the pros discovered the lures were highly effective when fished with faster retrieves, or when slightly modified, as Zell did.

The pros tried to keep the Pop-R a secret, but that was impossible in tournament fishing, especially after the lure began playing major roles in competition success. This success led to magazine and newspaper publicity, and PRADCO reintroduced the lure, which is now available in three different sizes.

In my opinion, Pop-Rs and similar lures draw reaction strikes. I don't think bass really hit them out of hunger or because the lures make them mad. I think the fish are alerted by the pop-pop-pop sound coming right beside their stump or clump of grass and they simply take advantage of an opportunity to feed.

With the exception of fishing in clear water when the object is to draw fish up out of deep water, most topwater fishing should be done around cover. The advantage of using floating surface plugs is that they may be chugged or popped right to a target, then stopped, then started again. Most strikes occur within one to two feet of the targets.

For this reason, you can often use heavy line while fishing them. This is especially true with buzzbaits, where 20-pound-test monofilament is standard. With Spooks and Pop-Rs, slightly smaller lines, usually 14- or 17-pound-test, can be used without inhibiting their actions. In fact, these lines work better than lighter 10- or 12-pound-test lines.

TOPWATER LURE RODS

Rod choices for topwater lures can be critical. You'll need a rod with a fairly limber tip so you can cast the smaller lures well and work them properly, but because they tend to draw strikes from big fish, you also need plenty of midrod and butt strength to control those fish.

Some pros like the 5½-foot rods when working Spooks because this shorter length doesn't hit the water each time the rod is jerked down. With the Pop-Rs and the prop baits, a slightly longer rod works just fine. I like a 6½- or 7-foot rod, which takes up a lot of slack line each time I set the hook.

You're going to miss strikes when you fish topwater lures because you literally take the lure away from the fish before it has a chance to fully engulf it. One possible solution, especially with buzzbaits, is to make sure you use a rod with a limber tip—the rod flexes more as the bass pulls the lure down, giving you a better angle for a hook-set.

Another solution is to train yourself to wait an extra heartbeat before you do set the hook. You have to physically wait until you actually feel the fish on the lure. I don't like to tell anyone to slow down their hook-set, but with a topwater lure you really do need just a moment of hesitation.

During three days of fishing at Mexico's Lake Comedero, I caught six bass weighing more than 10 pounds, including one that weighed 13 pounds. I have to say it's one of the best big bass lakes I've ever fished.

14

GOING AFTER TROPHY BASS

Each year during the seminars I give throughout the country, someone invariably asks me about my most memorable fishing experience. Certainly, during nearly half a century of fishing, I have had too many memorable experiences to recount, so my answer has usually been the day I won the Texas Bassmaster Invitational tournament on Sam Rayburn, February 25, 1994.

Now, however, I have to change my answer to three days in April 2000, when my friend Jim Stroud and I traveled to Lake Comedero, Mexico to film an episode for Jim's television show, "Jim Stroud's Classic Adventures." During those three days, I caught six bass weighing more than 10 pounds, including one weighing an even 13 pounds. On one of those days I caught three of the 10 pounders, two more over 9 pounds, and lost two others at the boat that were at least that big. For the entire trip, Jim and I caught 40 fish over 8 pounds.

Like nearly every bass fisherman I've ever met, I like big fish, and until going to Mexico I had caught 35 bass weighing more than 10 pounds. The fish have come from lakes all over the South and on a number of different lures, but over the years, one fact has become very clear to me: big bass do not act like little bass. They're different in a lot of ways.

HOW THEY DIFFER

For example, and again with Lake Comedero being the exception, all of my big bass have been caught between 10 A.M. and 2 P.M., a four-hour period during which I had few if any other strikes.

Most of my big bass have also been slightly deeper than any smaller bass I caught in the same area. The average depth has been between four and about eight feet. It isn't much deeper, but on a per-fish basis, on each day that I caught a 10 pounder, I also caught smaller bass more shallow. The only exceptions I have found to this occur in the spring, when all the fish, big and little, are moving shallow to spawn.

None of my 10 pounders have come from pure underwater structure either, such as a channel break, hump, or even the sharp edge of a point. I have caught the majority of them in vegetation, especially lily pads. A lot have come from flooded bushes, and a couple from thick hydrilla and milfoil.

Perhaps the strongest defining feature about the big bass I've caught has been the fact all but one have come on large lures. That single exception occurred at

Mark Tyler caught this 14 pound, 9 ounce bass in California's San Joaquin River Delta, the heaviest bass ever caught in a B.A.S.S. tournament. He used a ¼-ounce black jig with a large plastic trailer.

Sam Rayburn Reservoir where I caught a 10-pounder on a jig. It's funny how in the pro tournaments we all consider a jig a "big fish" lure that we use when we're really trying to add weight to our limits, but in truth, very seldom do you hear about a 10-pound bass being caught on a jig. Again, the exception usually occurs in spring when some anglers use jigs for sight-fishing.

LURE CHOICES

With all of this in mind, then, my first advice to anyone wanting to catch a bass weighing 10 pounds or larger is to use a big lure. I like a 10-inch plastic worm rigged Texas-style with a ½-ounce sinker and 4/0 or 5/0 hook. Big bass on the average seem to like their lures presented slowly, and this is certainly one you can crawl at a snail's pace.

Another lure choice, and one a lot of fishermen enjoy using, is a big, tandem willowleaf spinnerbait. My preference is a ½- or ⁹⁄₁₆-ounce model, because you can cast it half a mile and then wind it back in a slow-rolling, gentle rise-and-fall retrieve. You can change the speed of your retrieve too. Reel fast to make the lure rise, then stop reeling to 'kill' the bait beside a bush or stump. As I mentioned earlier, spinnerbaits are among the most versatile lures available, and big bass will certainly hit them.

BIG BASS AND CRANKBAITS

I have also caught some 10-pounders on buzzbaits and other types of topwater lures, but if I really had to choose my personal favorite big-bass lure, it would probably be a big, slow-wobbling crankbait that dives down to about 12 feet. Most fishermen don't really consider crankbaits to be trophy bass lures, but believe me, they are.

I'd been a crankbait fisherman long before Jim and I went down to Mexico, but Comedero is filled with standing timber and shallow brush, so like most fishermen down there I started throwing a big spinnerbait and a 10-inch plastic worm. I caught a 10-2 on the spinnerbait, and a 10-4 and a 10-8 on the worm, but then I saw a big bass chasing a tilapia, a small perch-like fish that forms the major part of the bass diet down there.

That's when I changed to a Fat Free Shad crankbait, a big, bulky, deep-diving lure that I could get down deep quickly, then slow my retrieve. In less time than it takes to tell, three monsters, including bass we weighed at 10-12, 11-7, and 13-0 had walloped the big plug.

BIG BASS, BIG LURE

I'll be the first to admit that Lake Comedero is not your typical bass lake, but the "big bass, big lure" theory seems to hold true just about everywhere. In 1977 I participated in a joint American-Cuban fishing challenge tournament on Cuba's famous Treasure Lake. I caught a 10-pound, 2-ounce bass down there on a black surface spoon—with an 8-inch black worm attached as a trailer. That lure looked like a snake swimming through the grass, and sure enough, it fooled a big fish.

Some time ago Jim, who has fished all over the United States for the past 25 years, spent four years fishing specifically for big bass on South Carolina's Lake Greenwood. He documented every bass he caught, which one year included 15 fish over 9 pounds and 12 over 10. By far, the majority of those monsters hit either a big crankbait, a big topwater lure, or a 10-inch plastic lizard.

Why do big bass seem to prefer big lures? A lot of fishermen think big bass are lazy and don't want to use all their energy chasing a lot of small baitfish when they can make one ambush and get a larger meal. Maybe that's true. Scuba divers who have studied big bass tell me most of them are usually swimming decidedly slower than smaller fish.

FISHING FOR BIG BASS

During my guiding years at Santee-Cooper, I caught a number of trophy-sized bass, and was fortunate enough to have some of my clients catch some too. At the same time, I also saw a lot of mistakes that could have easily been avoided. Because your chances of catching a bass weighing 10 pounds or more are far less than they are for catching a 2-pounder, you need to be prepared for your opportunity when it comes.

The first thing is using the proper equipment. You need a strong rod— nothing less than a 6½- or 7-foot medium-heavy-action—and line to match. I've heard stories about fishermen catching absolutely huge bass on 8- and 10-pound-test line, but most of these catches come from deep, clear water that's free of brush and snags that would easily break such line. When I am fishing clear water and know there's a distinct chance for a whopper, I may use line as light as 12-pound-test just so the bass don't see it as well, but I'll still use a big lure.

Actually, with some of the new fishing line technology being developed by Stren, Berkley, Sugoi, and other manufacturers, today it's possible to use a small diameter line without sacrificing anything in strength. Fluorocarbon line offers this advantage, and it practically disappears entirely underwater. It's a little more expensive than monofilament, but I'm really impressed with what I've seen of fluorocarbon line so far, and use it a lot in tournaments.

TAKE YOUR TIME

Another thing to keep in mind about fishing for trophy bass is to give yourself time to catch one. On Santee-Cooper, we always suggested that clients devote three consecutive days to the task if they wanted a bass weighing 10 pounds or more. Even today, 30 years later, guides on Lake Fork in Texas and Lake Okeechobee in Florida also tell their clients to try to spend three straight days on the water.

Big bass can come on any cast, especially in lakes known for their populations of trophy fish, so be prepared! Use large lures and heavy tackle, and keep the net ready.

At the same time, you want to make sure you spend those three days in proven big-bass water. You want to go to a place that has a history of producing 10-pounders. Today, based on what I saw and experienced at Lake Comedero, I'd easily rank it the best trophy bass lake in the world at this time. Ron Speed, whose company "Ron Speed's Adventures" in Malakoff, Texas, is the only agent serving Comedero, offers three- to five-day fishing packages. If you spend just three days there, I feel confident you'll have several chances at a big bass, and at the end of five days you'll probably be totally worn out. A few weeks before Jim and I fished there, another angler caught an 18-pounder.

WHERE THE TROPHIES ARE

Santee-Cooper still produces some 10-pounders, especially back in the Lake Marion swamps that don't receive much fishing pressure. In Florida, both Okeechobee and the Kissimmee Chain of Lakes (Tohopekaliga, Kissimmee, and the Kissimmee River) are capable of yielding a 10-pounder on any given cast. Lake Fork and Lake Ray Roberts in Texas have produced bass over 15 pounds, and in California, Clear Lake and the San Joaquin River Delta have also given up double digit bass that big. Clear Lake, in fact, produced a 17-pounder during the spring of 2000.

Regardless of where you go, however, you just can't ever tell what's going to happen when you set your sights on a trophy bass, because if there's anything predictable about big fish, it's that they're totally unpredictable.

PREDICTING THE UNPREDICTABLE

My close friend Steve Price, the co-author of this book with me, remembers a big-bass assignment in Florida for *Field & Stream* magazine several years ago. He and his guide were using live bait, and rigged three rods with golden shiners, the preferred trophy bass bait throughout the state. As they rigged the third rod and dropped the bait into the water, it went straight down and line started peeling off the reel. Steve set the hook and hauled in a 7-pounder. They'd been fishing 30 seconds, and all Steve had to do then was shoot his photos and he'd be finished.

They re-rigged that rod and began photographing. About 45 minutes later they noticed one of the rod tips bobbing a little, so Steve set the hook again. This time the fish weighed 10½ pounds.

Generally, it doesn't happen that easily. In fact, Steve can tell another story of fishing the same lake, Florida's Rodman Reservoir, as well as another nearby lake several years later and getting just one strike in three long, tedious days of fishing for a 10-pounder.

Sometimes, it seems you're just not meant to catch a big bass, particularly in a tournament where such a fish would usually mean lot of money. I remember practicing for the 1993 Texas Invitational on Sam Rayburn, where I was fishing a jig in an area of the lake known as the Black Forest. I'd had five bites one day but never set the hook on any of them when a local angler came up and told me I was in a pretty good spot.

Well, on the next bite I set the hook and nearly fell out of the boat when I saw the fish come to the surface. That bass weighed 12–4, and I quickly turned it loose after weighing it, hoping I could catch it again once the tournament started. The next day, however, the weather changed drastically, with plunging temperatures and a strong north wind that kept me from ever getting back to that spot for the entire tournament.

I can't explain why big bass act the way they do, and certainly not why they seem to change their personalities once they reach a certain size or age. All I can tell you is that they're wonderfully fun to try to catch, but that they're different.

Once you have turned professional, a boat and motor is just the beginning of a long list of basic equipment you'll need, all of which will cost money. You'll need to have some money in the bank when you start because you can't survive purely on tournament winnings from the start.

15

TURNING PRO

During the 1980 B.A.S.S. North Carolina Invitational at Albemarle Sound, I had a chance to win as we entered the final day of competition. The water had been rough all week and I'd really taken a pounding physically, since my fish were more than 40 miles away. On the last day, I made the long, difficult run once more, and caught a great stringer of bass I estimated would weigh nearly 20 pounds.

On the weigh-in stand, you can imagine my surprise when the scales showed only 16-15. I had been certain I had more than that. Then my heart sank as I realized I'd weighed in only six bass instead of the full limit of seven. I'd left a 3-pounder in my livewell, and once on the weigh-in stand, I could not go back to the boat and claim it. I finished fourth instead of a possible first, as I lost by about 3 pounds.

My mistake in not getting my entire catch to the scales was simply a mental error—I was physically and mentally exhausted from the week-long tournament. That's what competition at the highest level of professional fishing can do to you, and it happens to a lot of anglers.

In 1993 at Lake Texoma, Rick Clunn forgot what time he was due back at weigh-in and lost not only the heaviest stringer of the entire week but the tournament itself when he arrived late and was penalized. Larry Nixon, Denny Brauer, and other top pros can relate similar stories about what happens when you're exhausted from competition.

The mental stress is one of the most overlooked aspects of tournament fishing. Far too many ambitious young anglers look only at the glory that comes from winning: the money, the sponsorships, the seemingly carefree life of traveling and fishing. Believe me, there is far more to it than that.

In 1994-1995, I fished 11 national tournaments, each lasting seven days, including travel time. That made 77 days—more than two and a half months—I was away from my home and family. Although I didn't travel as far this season, I have put more than 50,000 miles on my truck traveling to and from tournaments in some years.

During that same 1993 Oklahoma Bassmaster Invitational where Rick Clunn forgot his weigh-in time, I finished second by just 7 ounces—and I lost two bass the final day that would easily have won for me.

In the Bassmaster Top 100 on the Connecticut River in September 1994, I accidentally bent my trolling motor on a rock 48 miles from the weigh-in site, and

I did not have a spare. Fortunately, a local gentleman loaned me his boat and I was able to continue fishing, but the results could have been far worse.

In short, when you fish professionally, you have to be prepared to take the bad with the good, because you're going to have plenty of both.

HIGH LEVEL OF COMPETITION

You're also going to encounter a different level of competition than you do in smaller tournaments. This is hard for inexperienced anglers to understand, but it's true. Instead of fishing against others who fish only on weekends, you'll be matching casts with full-time pros who don't do anything except fish, and they've been doing it for years. Once competition begins, they'll respect you as a fisherman and as a person, but they won't do you many favors.

That's why I think anyone who has dreams of someday becoming a full-time professional bass fisherman should not be in such a hurry to fish national tournaments. The first step should be to join a local bass club where it's possible to learn from the other club members in a much more relaxed atmosphere.

Make no mistake about it: club competition can be stiff, but it will help prepare you for what lies ahead. Five friends and I started a bass club in 1973 and stayed in it 13 years. On many nights before our tournaments I'd have trouble sleeping because I knew each of them wanted to beat me as much as I wanted to beat them, but it was all in fun and each of us became a better angler because of it.

If, after a period of club competition, you still want to fish professionally, then I suggest you enter one of the national events. If possible, pick a lake close to your home, or at least a lake you may have fished previously. If it's nearby, you'll reduce your expenses and you may be able to spend additional time on the water before the official cut-off date.

You can also fish a regional tournament trail, such as Anglers Choice or The Fisherman's Circuit, both of which offer weekend events with excellent prizes. Some of the national pros fish these events when schedules permit, so they're good training grounds for you.

THE ECONOMICS OF TURNING PRO

Fishing professionally is not cheap, and if you're totally without sponsorship, money will be one of your biggest considerations. In 2000-2001, the entry fee to fish a B.A.S.S Invitational was $600. To this, you can add at least $500 to $1,000 more for motel accommodations, meals, boat and vehicle gasoline, and other expenses. If you finish in the top 50 in the tournament, you might break even on your expenses.

Financial worries derail a lot of good fishermen simply because they're concerned about money and can't concentrate on their fishing. Many of today's top pros have gone through severe financial difficulties in which they were forced to

Most tournament pros I know have enough spare rods, reels, and lures to open a tackle store if they so desired. The reason for having so much equipment, however, is to be able to handle any emergencies or changes in conditions that may arise once competition begins.

sleep in their vehicles and eat one meal a day. Recently, I saw one competitor who ran out of gas during a tournament simply because he was trying to save money by not filling up his tank.

I think the experience of Texas fishing pro Jay Yelas offers a good example of how someone today can successfully break into professional fishing. While in college, Jay fished club tournaments. Then, for two full years after graduation, he fished bass tournaments in the western U.S., living out of his van to keep his expenses at a minimum, and most importantly, learning how to compete.

Yelas spent time on the water, gaining invaluable experience about fishing under many different conditions. Along the way he won his share of events and eventually caught the eye of several sponsors. After two years, he moved to Texas to compete on the national Bassmaster Tournament Trail, where he has done extremely well.

Because money will be one of your major considerations when you begin fishing professional tournaments, I think it's very important to have something in the bank before you start. I held a full-time job at Carolina Freight when I began fishing national tournaments. I took my allotted four weeks of vacation during tournaments and my supervisors allowed me to pay others to work for me the additional two weeks I needed to compete.

Something else you're going to need is a supportive family. More than a few marriages have been broken because of the financial drain as well as the continued separations. Some anglers take their families to the tournaments but this is difficult, especially after children enter school.

My wife, Pat, has always been totally supportive of me, and I can't tell you how comforting it has been. For 20 years she has looked after the family affairs as well as raised our two children while I've been away.

Something else many anglers don't always consider as thoroughly as they should when they begin fishing professionally is the amount of basic equipment they'll need. Of course, there are the obvious items, such as a boat, motor, trailer, and tow vehicle, but these aren't all.

You'll also need rods and reels, lures, fishing line, spare trolling motor, spare boat prop, battery charger, repair tools, and foul weather clothing. This investment alone can easily be as much as $3,500, to go with the $40,000 to $50,000 you may have in the boat, motor, and tow vehicle.

GET THE BEST EQUIPMENT YOU CAN AFFORD

In my seminars I stress to anglers to purchase the best equipment they can afford. Instead of owning 10 rods and reels that might or might not perform a full tournament season, I'd rather have four sets I know will work. Remember, your job is to catch fish; you won't have time to be repairing rods or reels each evening.

Most rod and reel contracts I know about today will allow an angler 10 sets per year. You can do with less. I have four rods I use in nearly all my fishing: a

Fishing is only part of the job of being a professional angler. During a tournament you will often be spending one or more evenings making special appearances for your sponsors.

pitching/flipping/crankbait rod, a heavy worm/jig rod, a medium-action spinnerbait rod, and a light spinning rod. In competition I carry these, as well as a spare of each.

I probably take more tackle than anyone else to tournaments, but I do it for a reason. I don't want to have to rush to a local tackle shop to purchase something I might need. I bring a case of fishing line containing bulk spools of everything from 6- to 30-pound-test. I probably take 1,000 crankbaits and 500 spinnerbaits, and I usually take 20 rods. There's a reason for this madness, especially where the lures are concerned. In the boat I may have 300 of those crankbaits and 100 spinnerbaits. I'm not worried about losing lures when I snag one; in fact, I don't even try to retrieve them when they do snag because I might spook fish when I do. After all, I made the cast to a spot where I believed a bass might be.

I keep a spare trolling motor in one rod box. It's a hand-control model, although I regularly use a foot-control model. The reason the spare is a hand-control model is it can be installed in just a couple of minutes whereas a foot-control unit takes much longer to replace. I think any angler can get by for a day with a hand-control troller.

I also have a special duffel bag with cold weather clothes. I fished a tournament in Florida years ago when the temperature fell to 40 degrees. Practically everyone froze, including me, so I make it a rule never to travel anywhere without insulated

If you're thinking of becoming a full-time professional, consider fishing club and local tournaments first. Then, try to fish a national tournament close to home to keep travel time and expenses to a minimum.

underwear, a snowmobile suit, gloves, and a helmet. I may not use them, but I enjoy the peace of mind that comes from knowing I have them if I need them.

If you don't have a quality rain suit in the boat with you, you're asking for trouble. Really good rain suits are expensive, but when you need one, nothing else will do. The majority of our tournaments are held rain or shine, and it's amazing how many times we encounter rain. What's bad about fishing in the rain is knowing you have to go out in it day after day.

You'll certainly need a good battery charger. I have one of the latest 20-amp chargers from AC Delco that charges both my trolling motor batteries quickly and simultaneously. I plug it in each evening when I return to my motel room and forget about it, knowing all my batteries will be fully charged by morning.

THE DAY STARTS EARLY

In competition, my day begins at 4:45 A.M. I get up this early so I don't have to rush to do anything. I get my boat in the water early and meet my partner for the day, then I may actually wait in the boat 45 minutes before my number is called for the send-off.

After weigh-in that afternoon, I meet my next day's partner and discuss strategy. Then I load the boat back on the trailer, fill the tanks with gas, and return to my motel where I prepare my tackle for the next day. That evening I may have a special promotional appearance to make at a nearby boat dealer, or perhaps attend a meeting conducted by one of my sponsors. Hopefully, I can be in bed by 9:30 P.M.

That's the way a tournament week goes for me. Even though I try to establish a routine of doing everything the same way each day, you can expect some mental breakdowns to occur at times. Most of us have launched our boats without the drain plugs at one time or another, and I've locked my keys in both my truck and my trailer!

FISHING PARTNERS

One thing you won't have any control over in tournament competition is the partner you'll be paired with each day. It is critical that you and your partner get along well and work together, otherwise neither of you will have much success. I've been fortunate; in all my days of competition, I've only drawn one partner I did not like.

The standard policy is that either partner can demand a coin toss to determine whose boat is used, and that each fisherman is entitled to one-half of the day doing what he wants to do.

Once you're on the water, you may be fishing together but you're also fishing separately. This is where you have to develop your mental toughness. Your thoughts can't be on what your partner's lure is doing, but rather what yours is doing. You can't be looking around at each passing boat and wondering how Jim, Jane, or Joe is doing.

You have to learn to concentrate, to focus totally and completely on what you can do to catch more fish, not only for a few minutes or hours, but for three, four, or possibly five straight days. It's tough, but that's what professional bass fishing is all about.

16

OBTAINING SPONSORSHIPS

Of all the different aspects of professional bass fishing, perhaps none is more misunderstood than the role of corporate sponsorships. Companies, primarily within the fishing industry but occasionally from without, pay a fisherman to use their products, sometimes quite handsomely. For a successful angler, these sponsorships provide the bulk of his annual income—the money that allows him to continue fishing.

What far too many fishermen do not realize is that tournament fishing success is not the primary reason companies hire anglers. Companies hire bass fishermen to promote and sell their products, so in effect, they become a field representative of that company.

What this means, simply, is that today's corporations look for anglers who can communicate well, who present a neat personal appearance, and who have the potential to achieve publicity for their products. Most corporations also have their own "personality" as well, so they look for a fisherman who can fit into that personality.

Corporations also look for anglers who have earned the respect of their peers. Again, this does not necessarily mean you have to be a tournament winner, but rather, a solid competitor who treats others with respect. When you get along well with your competition, you'll generally get along with the public.

The fishing industry is not only a small industry but also a highly competitive one, so most companies are also very concerned about loyalty. They're looking for someone willing to make a commitment to them and their products. Fishermen who continually change sponsors quickly lose their credibility not only with the industry but also with the public.

That's why it is so important for a fisherman to establish his own preference in boats, motors, rods, reels, lures, and accessories before he ever attempts to gain a sponsorship. If you don't honestly believe the equipment you're using is the very best available, how can you promote it as such?

Obtaining sponsorship today is not easy. Not only do corporations have limited sponsorship positions available, anglers who get these positions tend to keep them for many years. Bass fishing isn't like tennis or football where an athlete often retires by the time he's 35. I'm 60 and I've had some of my sponsorships more than a decade, and I plan to keep fishing competitively as long as I can.

There are several different ways to work with a boat company to receive sponsorship. Many anglers begin with a "memo bill" arrangement in which the package must be paid for after 12 months.

GOOD SPONSORSHIPS ARE OUT THERE

This is not to say you can't get good sponsorship, because you can. Every corporation in the fishing industry is always willing to consider a new angler if they feel he has skill and ability to successfully promote their products. Fishing sponsorships are a budget line item, and when a company wants to hire someone, they adjust their budget to bring him on board.

There are definitely right ways and wrong ways to begin your sponsorship search. My friend Gary Dollahon, the former public relations manager for Zebco, once told me he received 35 to 50 requests for sponsorship each week, but that only 5 to 10 percent of these were truly professional proposals. Many, he said, were totally generic, addressed "Dear Sir," and never mentioned specific products by name. On several occasions he had read the same proposal three times, as the fisherman sent one copy to Zebco and additional copies to Zebco's Browning and MotorGuide divisions! That's definitely the wrong way to try to obtain a sponsorship.

A sports writer once related another incident to me that really makes me wonder how some fishermen obtain any sponsorship at all. An angler who had just won a national bass tournament called this writer to make sure he would mention the name of a spinnerbait used in winning the tournament. When the writer asked for the company's location, the fisherman didn't know. Not only that, the fisherman wasn't even sure of the company's name!

When I want to approach a company for possible sponsorship, I first attempt to visit with them personally, either at a tournament, a boat show, or possibly even a seminar. This is primarily to introduce myself and to inquire if I can send them a resume for possible future sponsorship consideration. This is usually a brief visit, and I certainly do not discuss any possible contract terms.

In two decades of professional fishing, no company has ever refused to receive my resume. The first thing a company wants to see from any prospective employee is a resume; sometimes they file it for future reference and other times I'm sure they throw it away.

YOUR PRESENTATION MUST BE PROFESSIONAL

To keep them from throwing away my resume, I present it as professionally as possible. The very first thing I tell them is what I believe I can do for them, not what I want from them. This includes my general schedule in doing promotions, and an outline of my work with writers, television appearances, and especially my affiliations with local boat, motor, and tackle dealers.

I also include an overall synopsis of my career as a professional angler, as well as copies of magazine and newspaper articles in which I have been featured. If I know I will be appearing as a guest on a future television program, I provide the date so the company may be able to watch, if they desire. I also have letters of recommendation or of appreciation for special work I have performed for various organizations who do not necessarily sponsor me.

Here Jim Hladnik of Outboard Marine Corporation and I discuss outboards during a public appearance I made for the company one evening. Any sponsorship contract you have with a corporation will usually include several "free" days for appearances or other events such as this.

Basically, my resume includes a complete look at who I am and the type of work I can do.

Don't be discouraged if you don't hear from a company for several weeks after you submit your resume. The wheels of business often turn slowly. In the meantime, I suggest you start sending the company a very professionally prepared synopsis each month of what you've accomplished. This can include news of tournaments you've fished, any public appearances you may have made for any company, magazine or newspaper articles that feature your activities, or radio and television appearances.

KEEP AT IT

Again, do not give up if even this effort fails to bring a response. Just keep doing it, but by all means, make it as professional as possible. Believe it or not, if the company is at all interested in you, they have started a file that includes not only your resume, but each report you submit. A lot of things happen at corporate level to delay sponsorship decisions, so be patient.

Eventually, the company will ask for a personal meeting or interview. This can take place at a tournament, at corporate offices, or anywhere it may be convenient for you to meet. This meeting is the first time sponsorship money or products are specifically discussed.

When you are just beginning your fishing career, you'll probably only be offered products in exchange for wearing the company's logo patch on your fishing shirt or jacket. With rods and reels, you may receive as many as 10 sets to use over the next 12 months; with lures you'll probably get as many as you want, within reason.

Several arrangements may be considered when you approach a company for a boat and motor. Probably the most common is known as a "memo bill," in which you get free use of a boat for 12 months. Then the company sends you a bill for it. You have the option of paying for it yourself, or selling it and pocketing any profit you may have after paying the company. Normally, the price asked on a "memo bill" is discounted slightly.

WORK WITH A LOCAL DEALER

A second and better arrangement is one worked through your local dealer. Whenever you approach Outboard Marine Corporation (OMC), Mercury, or Yamaha, the first question you'll be asked is who your local dealer is. If you don't already have a good working relationship with a dealer, your chances of getting a product usually range between slim and none.

The policy with the OMC Boat Group is for your dealer to approach the boat company (in bass fishing this will be Stratos, Javelin, or Hydra Sports) for you. If OMC feels you can help them, they will memo a boat/motor package to the dealer who then turns it over to you. Twelve months later, the dealer gets the boat back to sell for as much profit as he can make. Everyone benefits from a situation like this. You receive a free boat for a year; the dealer gets a boat to sell; and OMC sells another boat to a dealer, plus gets added product visibility from you.

In years past, before both OMC and Mercury began buying different boat companies, anglers often had to arrange sponsorship deals like this for each component: one for a boat, another for an engine, another for trolling motor and accessories, and possibly even another for rigging the boat. Today, it's much easier and the boat and motor companies prefer it.

SALARY OR RETAINER ALSO NEEDED

Receiving products but not financial compensation only goes so far, however, and in time you'll need to start receiving a salary or retainer from some of your sponsors if you want to continue fishing professionally. Do not expect to make your living from tournament winnings.

How much should you ask? That depends on your stature and record as a professional fisherman, as well as on the size of the company. Today, I charge a company a minimum of $5,000 annually just to use their product and wear one of their patches on my shirt. As a beginner in the sport, don't expect to get a lot of help financially, but don't hesitate to consider negotiating either.

Any contract you have with a sponsor will generally include several "free" service days for them. These can be days when the company wants you to be present for a store opening or perhaps to do a seminar. You don't get paid extra for these days, only your expenses are covered. In my contracts, I have two to four of these free days, and I specify that any special meetings or filming days (such as for television commercials) count.

In my opinion, one of the most important aspects of sponsorship is keeping the sponsor informed of my activities. Each month I prepare a report of everything I've done in professional fishing for the past 30 days. This includes a listing of tournament competitions, public appearances, writer and television interviews, and copies of stories that may have been published. I prepare this report in a professional format, then make 19 separate copies and send one to each of my sponsors.

How important is this? Probably more important than you'd ever imagine, particularly when corporate budgets are being considered for a new year. If they have a full file on your activities but only a page or two from other anglers, you've increased your chances for a contract renewal considerably.

IMPORTANCE OF LOYALTY

As I have mentioned, loyalty is very important. From time to time you probably will change sponsors, but when you do, make certain you do it professionally. Don't break a contract, and don't burn any bridges, because you may have to cross them again in the future.

When you are hired by a sponsor, your concern should be how you can sell that sponsor's products. As a professional bass angler, you have a great deal of influence on the buying public, so you should make certain you totally believe in the products you use and endorse.

Let me give you a personal example. Mercury was my outboard engine sponsor for 14 years, even though I was running a Stratos boat for many of those years. Then, Mercury bought Astro and Procraft, while OMC bought Stratos. Even though there was never any pressure on me to change boat or motor companies, I elected to change from Mercury to Evinrude. In 1996, when Earl Bentz left Stratos to start Triton Boats, I resigned from Stratos and followed him to Triton.

I did this primarily as loyalty to Earl Bentz, the founder of Stratos boats, because I was the first pro Earl hired when he started the company in 1983. Earl, in fact, is largely responsible for my being able to leave Carolina Freight as a loading supervisor and become a full-time B.A.S.S. pro. I explained this to Mercury, who understood my decision completely; I did not make it a money issue at all, and to this day I have remained close friends with the Mercury organization.

The largest sponsorship contract I know of in bass fishing is about $100,000 annually, which includes several additional boats and motors in addition to a monthly salary. Contracts this big, however, are rare and don't come until you've proven yourself not only as an angler but also as salesman.

Many young anglers ask me about the usefulness of agents in bass fishing. Some fishing companies refuse to negotiate with agents but a handful of anglers today do use agents and they have realized a few new contracts because of the association. My honest opinion is that professional bass fishing as a sport is not big enough for agents now.

SEMINARS

As a professional angler, you'll also have the opportunity to make money by giving seminars. Daily fees for this range from $500 to as much as $1,500 per day for some well-known stars. I make 35 to 40 seminar appearances annually, usually between January and mid-April—and it can get hectic and tiring at times. In February 2000, for example, I did seminars in five states in five days. I came home for a few days then did seven more seminars in the next 12 days.

Various agencies and organizations produce the seminars, and often they call one of the tackle industry companies to see who might be available for an appearance. Once you become established on the "seminar circuit," you can often stay as busy as you want to be. In 1994, I made $112,000 from my sponsors and from seminar fees.

At the same time, my tournament winnings totaled $77,000, which included my win in the Texas Bassmaster Invitational at Sam Rayburn Reservoir in Texas. My travel and fishing expenses that year totaled $38,000, which gave me net earnings (from tournaments) of $39,000. Had I not won the Rayburn event, my expenses would likely have been greater than my winnings, which is why obtaining and keeping good sponsorships is so important in your career as a tournament fisherman.

17

MENTAL ATTITUDE: YOUR MOST IMPORTANT TOOL

During the 1977 Bass Masters Classic on Florida's Lake Tohopekaliga, a sudden cold front turned the fishing into an endurance contest. Eventual winner Rick Clunn had eight strikes the second day and boated two fish, then only two strikes the final day. He caught both of those bass too, and although one was too small to keep, the other weighed 2 pounds, 12 ounces and gave him the victory.

That made two consecutive Classic wins for Rick, which is quite an accomplishment, but to this day I personally am more impressed with how he won. Think about it for a moment: two faint, almost imperceptible worm bites in grass in eight hours with the world championship of bass fishing at stake. How do you keep going during all those hundreds of fruitless casts? How do you maintain such a high level of concentration for hours so you do feel a strike when it finally comes?

I wasn't a competitor in that 1977 Classic, but I've been in others that were equally as tough, and I can tell you the above questions are easy to answer but very difficult to achieve. What it takes is simply keeping a positive attitude—a firm, overriding belief that eventually a bass will strike and when it does, you're going to catch it. With this you must have a feeling of self-confidence that you're in the right area and using the proper lure and presentation.

When you have these, you have the most important tools in bass fishing.

BELIEVE IN WHAT YOU'RE DOING

In its broadest sense, this is the psychology of bass fishing, and it really is not different from any other sport or business. You have to believe in what you're doing, and believe you can do it, before you'll truly be successful.

At no time is this ever an instantaneous process and especially not in bass fishing. That's because there are always too many variables over which you have absolutely no control, such as weather conditions, the water quality, or the mood of the fish. Ironically, it is repeated experiences with these variables that can lead you to the positive attitude you need.

In short, gaining self-confidence and a positive attitude comes from spending time on the water so you develop a memory bank of experiences to draw from when you encounter these and other less than favorable conditions. What you

Even if you've had a bad day on the water, you're still a hero to some. Keeping a positive attitude is important. Something as simple as signing an autograph for a young fan should help build your confidence.

strive for is to build up enough positive experiences so you can react easily to the conditions without letting them discourage you.

At the same time, you can't let negative experiences rule your fishing. You have to learn from them, then put them out of your mind.

My close friend and well-known competitor Denny Brauer is a perfect example of how to do this. Brauer was once asked by a writer to describe a close call, how he'd narrowly missed winning a particular tournament several years earlier. Brauer refused to be interviewed on the subject, stating that he didn't dwell on negatives and had forgotten the entire event!

Believe me, this is not easy. One reason is because it is much easier to be discouraged in the face of adversity than encouraged. Thus, you're likely to encounter more "sour grapes" attitudes than smiling faces among your friends and competitors, and their attitudes can influence you if you let them. The popular saying that misery loves company is definitely true.

This is one reason some professional anglers stay by themselves, away from the headquarters at tournaments. They rent quiet cottages or even camp, rather than stay at the Holiday Inn. It's not because they're antisocial; they're just trying to stay away from negative influences that can make it difficult for them to keep a positive attitude.

Another reason thinking positive is so difficult is because it's going to take you some time to build up that bank of positive experiences in bad conditions. You might get lucky and find some active bass in cold, muddy water at your very first stop, but it doesn't happen often.

Even time on the water, however, does not provide the complete answer to gaining self-confidence. What it takes is time on the water alone that forces you to make all the decisions that come in a day of fishing. Believe me, nothing builds confidence faster than actually catching a bass—except catching a bass on a big lake by yourself. That is how you build that memory bank of experiences.

Do you remember your first attempt at driving an automobile, how nervous you were during the test for your driver's license? The nervousness was caused by a lack of experience—you had little confidence because there was no bank of positive memories upon which to draw. Until you applied for your license, all the automobile driving had been done for you by someone else.

Fishing is exactly the same.

The key to making all this work for you is in making every trip on the water a positive learning experience. Even when you do poorly, you can learn from it by studying what a more successful fisherman did. This is why many fishermen have fishing diaries and others keep detailed computer records of tournament results. Looking back, they can study how fish reacted under specific conditions and what it took to catch them. There are even professional computer programs available now that aid you in doing this.

To make such an experience truly meaningful, you have to seriously compare what you did that was unsuccessful against what was successful. Sometimes this

Nothing builds confidence more in fishing than catching fish, and when you win a national tournament, it helps even more. Here I pose after winning the 1994 Texas Bassmaster Invitational on Sam Rayburn.

takes some real soul-searching too, but always remember that no matter how bad the conditions are in a tournament, someone is going to win even if he only catches one fish, which, by the way, has actually happened!

FOLLOW YOUR FEELINGS

Another subtle key to gaining self-confidence is learning to listen to and obey your intuitions. Some call intuition their "gut feelings," or describe it as "a little bird told me . . ." I honestly don't know what intuition really is and I can't give you a scientific description of it but I can say that everyone has intuition and it is always correct. The problem all of us have is listening to it.

This is where fishing alone becomes so important. The next time you're on the water and "a little bird" tells you to move out to that point and try a deep crankbait, do it. Don't spend time second-guessing yourself, just go. Now, once you're on that point you still have to decide exactly how and where to fish it but just imagine the confidence boost you'll get when you do catch bass.

How many times have you been speeding down a lake and suddenly decided to fish a cove or particular area that you hadn't ever fished before? And how many times have you or your friends caught bass in such a place? It was intuition that took you there, and that's how positive it can be.

Let me give you another example from my friend Rick Clunn, who has probably studied this entire question of self-confidence and positive thinking more than any other bass fisherman I know. Rick was fishing the 1983 U.S. Open tournament on Lake Mead, Nevada, a pretty lake in the high desert near Las Vegas but not a particularly fertile lake. Big fish there (7-pounders) are pretty rare. The tournament has attracted many fishermen from throughout the U.S., however, because the winner's check is for $50,000.

The night before the final day of competition when he was pretty far down in 13th place, Rick's intuition told him to spend that next day more than 100 miles from the launch area, because there he'd catch the fish he needed to win. Rick had never fished the area (actually near the mouth of the Grand Canyon) before, but he followed his intuition and caught two 5-pounders there and won the tournament.

My own experience, both as a guide at Santee-Cooper as well as a tournament pro, have given me the same types of results, although not quite as dramatic as Rick's. Many times at Santee, something would tell me to move to a certain area to fish a particular log or grass bed, and invariably my clients or I would catch bass there. I didn't go to the log or grass because it looked good or had produced for me before. I simply went because I "had a feeling" that was the place to try. That's what your intuition is, and the more you let yourself listen to it, the stronger it will become.

Using your intuition works side by side with positive thinking, the belief you are going to catch a fish in a certain spot by using a specific technique. In the

Keeping a positive attitude on a slow day on the water isn't easy, but it is often what separates winners and losers. Many pros try to visualize what their lure is doing and imagine a fish hitting each time.

beginning as you start exploring this concept, thinking positively will probably have to be a very conscious effort.

I know many fishermen today, some of the best in tournament competition, who tell themselves on every cast "This is the one a bass will bite. This is when a fish is going to hit." Doing this helps keep your thoughts focused on your cast, and it also aids in trying to visualize what your lure is doing underwater. By the way, this is exactly what Rick did on that cold day on Lake Tohopekaliga.

POSITIVE VISUALIZATION

Positive visualization—thinking very precisely about what your lure is doing and how a bass is going to strike—is a training technique used in many sports today, especially in Olympic competition. Divers, for example, visualize each part of their routine, from climbing the ladder, walking down the board, springing into the air, making their twists and turns, and entering the water. In each visualization, the dive is perfect. In time, the diver begins to believe that's exactly how he's going to perform in competition, and more often than not, he does.

I have to emphasize here that all of the mental exercises I've described will not give you a shortcut to bass fishing success. You still must be able to match lure and place selection to seasonal patterns, and then be able to present your lure in the proper manner. You still have to develop the ability to see your line twitch as a fish hits your jig or feel the added weight of a bass on your Carolina rig in heavy grass.

But thinking positively and trying to visualize your lure's actions will make all the other aspects of bass fishing easier. Psychologists cannot fully explain why thinking positive works; they just know it does, and so do I.

So learn to believe in yourself by depending upon yourself, and you'll see your catches increase, even when you're fishing Lake Tohopekaliga after a cold front.

INDEX

A

ABF World Championship (1975) 4
Albemarle Sound 113
Angler of the Year 5, 6
Anglers Choice 114
attitude
  avoiding negative influences 131
  building up positive experiences 129, 131–32
  gaining self-confidence 129, 131–32
  positive visualization 135
  using your intuition 133, 135

B

Bagley, Jim 56, 77, 78
Barnes, Larry 29, 31
barometric pressure
  effect on bass behavior 37–39
  understanding atmospheric pressure 37
bass
  ability to detect vibrations 8
  adaptability of 9–10
  consistency of 10
  feeding habits 9
  importance of learning about 7, 13
  intelligence vs. instinct 7–8
  keeping an open mind as you learn 11
  lateral lines 8
  range of movement 12
  seasonal movement 12–13
  survival mechanisms 8
  visual abilities 8–9
  See also finding bass
B.A.S.S. MegaBucks tournament (1997) 84
B.A.S.S. North Carolina Invitational (1980) 113
Bassmaster Oklahoma Invitational (1992) 99
Bassmaster Oklahoma Invitational (1993) 113
Bassmaster Oklahoma Invitational (1994) 23, 25
Bass Masters Classic (1977) 129
Bass Masters Classic (1980) 6
Bass Masters Classic (1987) 11
Bass Masters Classic (1993) 91
Bass Masters Classic (1996) 84
Bass Masters Classic (1998) 84, 87
Bassmaster Top 100 (1994) 113–14
Bentz, Earl 127
Big Os 5, 89
Black Forest 16, 63, 110–11
blades, for spinnerbaits 55–56
boat docks, as bass locations 21–22, 22
Brauer, Denny 84, 87, 113, 131
Brewer, Charlie 73
Bush, George 5, 6
buzzbaits 98–99

C

Cajun Tackle 80
Carolina Freight Company 1–2, 6
Carolina rigs
  adapting to varying water conditions 78–79
  adding rattles or beads 80
  casting 81
  development of 78
  lizards 79, 80
  making 78
  using sinkers 80
Catawba River 2
Chancellor, Jack 78
Chapple, Paul 18
Cherryville, North Carolina 2
Cherryville Bassmasters 4
Chickahominy River 42
Choke Canyon Lake 13
Chug Bugs 98
chuggers 98
Clear Lake 110
Clunn, Rick 17, 47, 113, 129, 133
Cochran, George 11, 83, 84
Colorado blades, for spinnerbaits 55
Comedero, Lake 104, 105, 107
company sponsorships. See professional, becoming a
Connecticut River 113–14

Cook, Ken 8
cover
  bass preference for 10, 10
  hitting with lures 48
  crankbaits 35, 88, 92
  achieving the desired depth 89–90
  as cold-water lures 32
  deep cranking 95
  deep-diving in shallow water 94–95
  development of 5, 89
  feeling crankbaits 91, 93
  importance of wobble 90–91
  lipless 91
  as lures for trophy bass 107
  with rattles 91
  selecting rods for 93
  stand-still crankbaiting 93–94
  suspending lures 94
  varying your retrieve 95
  versatility of 89
  wide vs. tight wobble 90
crawling plastic worms 73–74
Creme, Nick 71
Cumberland, Lake 6

D

Dance, Bill 27, 59
Deaver, Lloyd 78
deep cranking 95
deep-diving crankbaits 94–95
defining a pattern 13
depthfinders, ability of bass to detect 8
Devil's Horses 98
docks, as bass locations 21–22, 22
Dollahon, Gary 123
Dowden, Bo 3
dropping spinnerbaits 59
drop-shotting 86

E

Eagles of Angling tournament 5
Eaker, Earl 2
Eaker Shaker blades 85
Estep, Mike 5
Evinrude 127

F

fan-casting 48
feeding habits 9
finding bass
  confidence areas
  criteria for 15
  large spawning flats as 17
  major tributaries as 16
  small, inaccessible creeks as 16–17
  tips for identifying 16
  upper reaches of lakes as 16
  using maps to locate 15–16
  fishing to your strength 16–17, 19
  importance of timing 19
  marking your map 17
  matching seasonal patterns to lake sections
    17–19
  observing wildlife activity 20
  recommended locations
  boat docks 21–22, 22
  main lake pockets 27, 28
  points 23–25, 24
  riprap 23
  vegetation 25–26, 26, 28
  trying the next option 19
  watching the variables 19
  working from deep to shallow 25
  See also water, bodies of; weather, impact of
finesse fishing 83
Fisherman's Circuit 114
Fish Finders 78
fishing to your strength 16–17, 19
Fite, Randy 31
flipping lures 46, 50, 50–51
flipping to the south 6
floating worms 75, 77
Fork, Lake 31, 110
Fritts, David 91, 93

G

Garland, Bobby and Gary 83
Garrett, Doug 83, 84
Gitzits 83
Gliebe, Dave 1, 5–6
glitter skirts 61

Grand Lake 99
Greenwood, Lake 108

H
Hill, Loren 27
Hladnik, Jim 124
hopping jigs 65, 67
Houser Hell Divers 54
hydrilla 16

I
Ingram, Charlie 5
instinct, vs. intelligence 8
intuition, using 133, 135

J
jigs 32
  best colors for 70
  choosing the correct weight 63–65, 64
  as cold-water lures 31, 32, 32–33
  determining rate of fall 63–65, 64
  developing lure awareness 63
  head design 70
  hopping the jig 65, 67
  with rattles 70
  as second cast lures 71
  selecting rods for 70
  shaking the jig 67
  swimming the jig 67–68
  trailers for 70
  varying your retrieve 65, 67–68
  watching your line 65
  as year-round lures 68

K
Kissimmee, Lake 4, 110
Kissimmee Chain of Lakes 110
Kissimmee River 110
Klein, Gary 63, 98
Knight, John Alden 42
Knoxville, Tennessee 4–5

L
lake pockets, as bass locations 27, 28
large bass. See trophy bass, catching
lateral lines 8
lift, counteracting 56–57
lipless crankbaits 91

lure awareness, developing 63
lure presentation
  changing lures 47
  changing your retrieve angle 48, 50
  fan-casting 48
  flipping 46, 50, 50–51
  hitting the cover 48
  importance of being in the strike zone 45
  keeping your lure in productive water 45, 47
  pitching 46, 50, 51
  skipping 51–52
  varying retrieves 48

M
Mann, Tom 4, 74
maps
  marking 17
  using maps to identify confidence areas 15–16
Marion, Lake 96, 110
Martin, Lake 42
Martin, Roland 3, 4, 53
Martin, Tommy 68
Mead, Lake 133
Mercury 125, 126, 127
metabolism, effect of water temperature on 29, 31
metalflake skirts 61
milfoil 16
moon phases, effect on bass behavior 42–43
Morton, Jim 99
Moultrie, Lake 53
muddy water, effect on bass behavior 40
Murray, Lake 4–5

N
Nixon, Larry 83, 84, 113
Norman, Lake 3–4, 35
North Carolina State Championship 3–4
Northwest Bank 4

O
Ohio River 11
Okeechobee, Lake 33–34, 110
Outboard Marine Corporation (OMC) 125–26

P

Parker, Hank 58, 96
Pico Pops 101
pitching lures 46, 50, 51
Pixton, Dennis 72–73
Pixton rigs 72–73
P.J. Pops 101
plastic lizards 79, 80
plastic lures 79
plastic tube jigs 82
  advantages of 84–85, 86–87
  Carolina rigs 86
  development of 83–84
  drop-shot rigs 86
  power fishing with 83, 84
  rigging 85–86
  split-shot rigs 86
  spring use 81
  using Eaker Shaker blades 85
plastic worms 35, 72
  Carolina rigs 78, 80–81
  crawfish 79, 81
  crawling along the bottom 73–74
  craw-worms 79, 81
  development of 71
  floating worms 75, 77
  getting started 75
  Pixton rigs 72–73
  setting the hook 80
  Slider rigs 73
  Sosy Eels 77
  split-shotting 75
  Spring Tails 77
  swimming tails 77–78
  swimming worms 75, 77
  Texas rigs 71–72, 80
  using sinkers with 73, 80
  Wacky Worms 77
points, as bass locations 23–25, 24
Pop-Rs 98, 102–3
positive attitude. See attitude
positive visualization 135
power fishing 83
presentation, lure. See lure presentation
professional, becoming a
  author's experience 1–6
  competing locally first 114
  dealing with mental/physical exhaustion 113, 119
  example of Jay Yelas 116
  getting along with your partner 119–20
  getting equipment 116
  handling financial pressures 114, 116, 128
  importance of family support 116
  managing your time 119
  obtaining sponsorships
  approaching companies for sponsorship 123, 125
  asking for retainers 126
  being persistent 125
  difficulty of 121
  free service days 126
  importance of loyalty 121, 126–27
  keeping your sponsors informed 126
  memo bills for boats and motors 125
  role of sponsorships 121
  using agents 127–28
  working with local dealers 125–26
  presenting seminars 128
  taking equipment to tournaments 116–17, 119
  taking the bad with the good 113–14
prop baits 98

R

rain, effect on bass behavior 39–40
rattles, for jigs 70
Ray Roberts, Lake 110
retrieves
  changing the angle of 48, 50
  varying 48
  See also specific lures
riprap, as a bass location 23
RM Engineering 9, 21, 59
Rodman Reservoir 110
rods
  for crankbaits 93
  for jigs 70
  for spinnerbaits 55
  for topwater lures 103
Ron Speed's Adventures 110
Rook, Scott 83, 84
Rowland, Zell 102–3

S

Sam Rayburn Reservoir 16, 29, 63, 81, 110
San Joaquin River Delta 106, 110
scales, expelled 9
Scott, Robert Carey 71
seasonal movement
    matching seasonal patterns to lake sections
        17–19
    understanding 12–13
self-confidence. See attitude
Seminole, Lake 5–6
shaking jigs 67
skipping lures 51–52
skirt materials, for spinnerbaits 59, 61
Slap-Sticks 98
Slider rigs 73
slow rolling spinnerbaits 56
slush baits 98
snow, effect on bass behavior 42
Solunar Tables 42–43
sonar signals, ability of bass to detect 8
Sosy Eels 77
Speed, Ron 110
spinnerbaits 35
    adding trailers to 61–62
    as cold-water lures 32, 55
    counteracting lift 56–57
    development of 53
    dropping 59
    feeling blade vibrations 53, 55
    Houser Hell Divers 54
    importance of depth 59
    line for 62
    new skirt materials for 59, 61
    selecting 55
    selecting rods for 55
    slow rolling 56
    uniqueness of 53
    varying your retrieve 57
    for vegetation 55–56
    wire for 61
split-shotting 75, 86
sponsorships, corporate. See professional,
    becoming a
Spring Tails 77
St. Clair, Lake 86
stand-still crankbaiting 93–94

stick baits 98
Stratos boats 127
strike zones 45
Stroud, Jim 105, 107, 108
surface lures. See topwater lures
survival mechanisms 8
swimming lures
    jigs 67–68
    plastic worms 75, 77
    tails 77–78

T

Texas Bassmaster Invitational (1994) 16, 29
Texas rigs 71–72, 80
Texoma, Lake 23, 25
timing, importance of 19
Tiny Torpedoes 98
Tohopekaliga, Lake 110, 129
topwater lures
    buzzbaits 98–99
    chuggers 98, 101–3
    developing a routine 99, 101
    importance of 96–97
    popping chuggers 101–2
    Pop-Rs 98, 102–3
    prop baits 98
    selecting rods for 103
    slush baits 98
    stick baits 98
    tips for using 99
    types of 97–99
    uses for 96–97
    walking your lure 101
    Zara Spooks 98, 101
trailers
    for jigs 70
    for spinnerbaits 61–62
Treasure Lake 107–8
Triton Boats 127
trolling motors, leaving on 8
trophy bass, catching 104, 106
    allowing enough time 108, 110
    choosing lures 107–8
    recommended locations for 110
    unpredictability of 110–11
    using crankbaits 107
    using the proper equipment 108

vs. smaller bass 105, 107
Truman Lake 39
tube jigs. See plastic tube jigs
Tyler, Mark 106

U
U.S. Open tournament (1983) 133

V
vegetation, as a bass location 25–26, 26, 28
vibrations, ability to detect 8
visual abilities 8–9

W
Wacky Worms 77
water, bodies of
color of 16
considering the history of 16
looking for clear water 40
muddy 40
shallow
bass preference for 10
variables affecting bass presence in 10–11,
    13, 19
temperature
adapting your fishing to cold water 31
cold-water lures 31–33, 32
comfort zone for bass 29
effect on bass metabolism 29, 31
finding cold water in summer 34, 34–35
finding warm water in winter 33–34
fishing windy shorelines in the fall 35–36
as the greatest factor influencing bass
    behavior 29
impact of sudden changes in 29
understanding the dynamics of 11
weather, impact of
barometric pressure changes 37–39
heavy rains 39–40
muddy water 40
snow 42
wind 40–42, 41
Westmorland, Billy 89
wildlife, observing the activity of 20
Willowleaf blades, for spinnerbaits 55–56
wind, effect on bass behavior 40–42, 41
Wingate, Jack 44, 97, 99, 101

wobble, crankbait 90–91
Woodchoppers 98
Woodwalkers 98
worms. See plastic worms
Wylie, Lake 21

Y
Yamaha 125
Yelas, Jay 116
Young, Fred 5, 89
Young, Odis 89
Younger, Ken 1–2, 6

Z
Zara Spooks 98, 101
Zebco 123

ABOUT THE AUTHOR

Steve Price has been a full-time writer and photographer for more than two decades, specializing in fishing, outdoor travel, and wildlife photography. Assignments have taken him not only throughout the United States but also to Canada, Central and South America, the Caribbean, Africa, and Asia. He is considered one of America's premier freshwater fishing writers, and both his writing and photography have won international acclaim. This is Steve Price's sixth book. His previous books include *World Championship Bass Fishing* and the highly acclaimed *America's Best Bass Fishing*. His upcoming book will feature the best tips and techniques for bass fishing.

Guy Eaker is one of America's most highly respected competitive bass anglers as well as one of fishing's most popular personalities. He has won major events at all levels of the sport including the prestigious Tournament Trail of the Bass Anglers Sportsman Society where he has qualified for the Bass Masters Classic world championship 10 times. He has been privileged to fish with the president of the United States, not once but twice, and he has traveled throughout the United States and into several foreign countries as a spokesman for bass fishing. In his more than 20 years as a competitive fisherman he has also helped develop several new lures and assisted in the design of numerous others. He lives with his wife Pat in Cherryville, NC.

FALCON GUIDES® Leading the Way™

FALCON GUIDES® are available for where-to-go hiking, mountain biking, rock climbing, walking, scenic driving, fishing, rockhounding, paddling, birding, wildlife viewing, and camping. We also have FalconGuides® on essential outdoor skills and subjects and field identification. The following titles are currently available, but this list grows every year. For a free catalog with a complete list of titles, call FALCON® toll-free at 1-800-582-2665.

SCENIC DRIVING GUIDES

Scenic Driving Alaska and the Yukon
Scenic Driving Arizona
Scenic Driving the Beartooth Highway
Scenic Driving California
Scenic Driving Colorado
Scenic Driving Florida
Scenic Driving Georgia
Scenic Driving Hawaii
Scenic Driving Idaho
Scenic Driving Indiana
Scenic Driving Kentucky
Scenic Driving Michigan
Scenic Driving Minnesota
Scenic Driving Montana
Scenic Driving New England
Scenic Driving New Mexico
Scenic Driving North Carolina
Scenic Driving Oregon
Scenic Driving the Ozarks
Scenic Driving Pennsylvania
Scenic Driving Texas
Scenic Driving Utah
Scenic Driving Virginia
Scenic Driving Washington
Scenic Driving Wisconsin
Scenic Driving Wyoming
Scenic Driving Yellowstone and
   the Grand Teton National Parks
Scenic Byways East & South
Scenic Byways Far West
Scenic Byways Rocky Mountains
Back Country Byways

WILDLIFE VIEWING GUIDES

Alaska Wildlife Viewing Guide
Arizona Wildlife Viewing Guide
California Wildlife Viewing Guide
Colorado Wildlife Viewing Guide
Florida Wildlife Viewing Guide
Indiana Wildlife Vewing Guide
Iowa Wildlife Viewing Guide
Kentucky Wildlife Viewing Guide
Massachusetts Wildlife Viewing Guide
Montana Wildlife Viewing Guide
Nebraska Wildlife Viewing Guide
Nevada Wildlife Viewing Guide
New Hampshire Wildlife Viewing Guide
New Jersey Wildlife Viewing Guide
New Mexico Wildlife Viewing Guide
New York Wildlife Viewing Guide
North Carolina Wildlife Viewing Guide
North Dakota Wildlife Viewing Guide
Ohio Wildlife Viewing Guide
Oregon Wildlife Viewing Guide
Puerto Rico & the Virgin Islands
   Wildlife Viewing Guide
Tennessee Wildlife Viewing Guide
Texas Wildlife Viewing Guide
Utah Wildlife Viewing Guide
Vermont Wildlife Viewing Guide
Virginia Wildlife Viewing Guide
Washington Wildlife Viewing Guide
West Virginia Wildlife Viewing Guide
Wisconsin Wildlife Viewing Guide

HISTORIC TRAIL GUIDES

Traveling California's Gold Rush Country
Traveling the Lewis & Clark Trail
Traveling the Oregon Trail
Traveler's Guide to the Pony Express Trail

■ *To order any of these books, check with your local bookseller*
*or call FALCON ® at **1-800-582-2665**.*
Visit us on the world wide web at:
www.falcon.com

FALCON®

FALCON GUIDES ® Leading the Way™

www.Falcon.com

Since 1979, Falcon® has brought you the best in outdoor recreational guidebooks.
Now you can access that same reliable and accurate information online.

❐ <u>Browse our online catalog</u> for the latest Falcon releases on
hiking, climbing, biking, scenic driving, and wildlife viewing
as well as our Insiders' travel and relocation guides. Our online
catalog is updated weekly.

❐ A <u>Tip of the Week</u> from one of our guidebooks or how-to
guides. Each Monday we post a new tip that covers anything
from how to cross a rushing stream to reading contour lines on
a topo map.

❐ A chance to <u>Meet our Staff</u> with photos and short
biographies of Falcon staff.

❐ <u>Outdoor forums</u> where you can exchange ideas and tips with
other outdoor enthusiasts.

❐ Also <u>Falcon screensavers and panoramic photos</u> of spectacular
destinations.

And much more!

*Plan your next outdoor adventure at our web site. Point your browser to
www.Falcon.com and get FalconGuided!*

FALCON®